W0018092

THE
ART
OF
SELLING

LEFTERIS
PAPAGEORGIOU

FiNGERPRINT!

Published 2024

FiNGERPRINT!

Prakash Books

Fingerprint Publishing

@FingerprintP

@fingerprintpublishingbooks

www.fingerprintpublishing.com

Copyright © 2024 Prakash Books

Copyright Text © Lefteris Papageorgiou

All rights reserved. No part of this publication may be reproduced, stored in a retrieval system or transmitted in any form or by any means, electronic, mechanical, photocopying, recording or otherwise (except for mentions in reviews or edited excerpts in the media) without the written permission of the publisher.

The views and opinions expressed in this book are solely those of the author. The facts presented were reported as true by the author at the time of publication. The publisher assumes no responsibility for their accuracy or veracity and is not liable for any errors, omissions, or consequences arising from the use of the information. References to third-party products, services, or websites are for informational purposes only and do not constitute endorsements.

ISBN: 978 93 6214 757 8

To my wife, Dimitra, the only person
who can sell me anything.

Contents

The purpose of business is to create and keep a customer.

Peter Drucker

Author's Note

Finally, you're in the conference room.
You have just finished your presentation—the so-called pitching—and your partner is answering questions.

You reflect for two seconds, and you think you probably did well.

Now, you're waiting for the answer. And you know that no matter how extensive your language is, only two words matter—yes and no.

You remember, it all started a couple of weeks ago when a friend handed you a business card and told you to give them a call.

"I think you'll be able to do business together."

And now you've done your best. You covered all the information about the product, your company, and closed the presentation at the right time. Basically, you followed the rules you knew would work. After mentoring, watching countless YouTube videos, plowing through books, and rehearsals in front of the mirror, you got the job done.

Now, you wait. The people around you have no idea what you're thinking. As time goes by, you have second thoughts.

'Should I have made the presentation more detailed? Should I have given more technical details about the product?

Should I have done more research about the company?

Did I do anything wrong? And if so, what was my mistake?'

You go over it in your head repeatedly for the next few days. Unintentionally and for no reason, you start leaning toward no rather than yes. You remember the mistakes you made, the answers you could have given in more detail, and maybe your body language was wrong during the discussion.

They thank you for the presentation.

"We'll get back to you in a couple of days," they say.

A week passes by.

And then, the phone rings. You realize from the caller ID that it's *them*.

You take a deep breath . . . and exhale half of it. You recall how to make a poker face from a Robert Redford movie. No grimacing, even if you can't be seen on the phone. You read somewhere that the tone of your voice reflects your mood.

"Hello . . ."

 Nothing happens until a sale is made.

Anonymous

This is not a typical book about sales. It's not an essential tool for the experienced salesperson, though they, too, could use help to put their thoughts in order.

This is not one of the hundreds of sales books that explain how to increase your revenue from five million to 50 million. That's a different kind of problem. This book is for the start-up founder. For the person who is the CEO, CFO, the salesperson, and the one who pays the bills at the end of the month, all at the same time.

This book is written for you. The person who established a start-up with the right foundations, found the product, the market it addresses, the customer it appeals to. Now, the moment has come to transition to the next phase: selling it.

Introduction

I come from a family where we never discussed entrepreneurship or what it takes to develop a business perspective. We never had anything to do with sales.

However, I found a job as a furniture salesman. I was studying at university at the time. I was trained in the store by an older salesman, and gradually got used to the role. Nowadays, this probably wouldn't be enough. I was a likeable young man who, after finding out what the customer was looking for, did his sales pitch and moved on to the next. If the customer wanted to, they would buy.

Next, I got a job at a radio station as a broadcaster and I was introduced to the clients of its advertising department. The radio shows assured the client I knew what I was talking about and that the information I presented was correct.

They could see I was part of the sector, was commercially aware, and therefore, knew what would help.

A few months later, I was the head of the radio station's advertising department. In the evenings, I closed screening deals in bars and restaurants in Thessaloniki, and during the day, I broadcast shows and recorded commercial spots.

After graduating from university, I had to serve in the army in Greece, so for 18 months, my life was put on hold.

While I was waiting to get back to work and be able to cover my expenses again, I met a friend who played in a band.

This was a group of talented guys with great potential. So, I took on the management of the band.

The following months were amazing.

As the band improved, I booked gigs for them at various entertainment venues and municipal events. In northern Greece at first, and then in the southern part of the country and on the islands. The team was flying high.

At the same time, I got a job as the head of the technical department in Fibran, one of the largest insulating material manufacturers in Europe, established in more than 25 countries today. My job was to present the company's products to engineers all over Europe. A salesman effectively, disguised as a consultant.

At the end of 1998, I got the members of the band together and set them a target to double the number of concerts and sign an agreement with a record company in the following year. I would step down after that, and they would have to find someone to replace me. They looked at me in surprise. It was the first time they'd made so many appearances. We were going to be doubling them? And then release an album in the same year? It all sounded a bit far-fetched.

On the other hand, I knew what needed to be done. I broke it down into individual tasks and lined up the dominoes.

In 1999, we performed 75 concerts. A record number, not only for our band, but for any band in Greece.

At the beginning of the year 2000, we signed our first record contract. On March 22, 2000, the first presentation took place. Huge crowds of people and journalists were present. Well-known artists referred to the band. Two songs from the album made it to the Top 10 on radio stations across Greece and on various Greek radio stations around the world.

Everything happened as per the plan.

At the dinner that followed, I said goodbye to the band.

Now, I had to apply myself as a civil engineer. Like everyone else, I started with permits and licenses and very quickly moved on to renovations and private construction projects. Work was going amazingly well. Sales, in this case, were different, but for me the context was very clear: I had to convince the customers to trust me and close the deals.

Over the next decade, I founded 13 more companies in five countries: in construction, commercial, and renewable energy, and one company in the food packaging sector.

In 2008, I came across statistics stating the engineering industry would be short of work for the next 10 years. It was then that I founded Entranet.

The scene changed. I had to appeal to the global market and look for clients and investors. The crisis, however, had begun and the Greeks, at that stage, had the worst brand name in the history of Hellenism.

With confidence, I got on with the job I had known the best. But this time, things were different. Every meeting was difficult to arrange and costly. Nine times out of 10, the emails we sent out did not receive a response. The products we considered exceptional were not acknowledged to the same degree in the marketplace.

At the same time, we started presenting Entranet to investors. There was a storm of rejections. No one said our product was bad, or that business plan required changes. Everyone congratulated us on our business and our products. But I wasn't closing any deals. I couldn't convince the investment community to fund our efforts. I was doing something wrong.

At a meeting with investors in the USA amid very tight competition, I received the public award but failed to get the investors' award.

So, I was able to sell the product but couldn't get the message across to investors. But when you need the investors' money to go to production, having your product accepted commercially is of little importance. Finally, after 200 presentations to investors, individuals, and institutions on both sides of the Atlantic, we reached an agreement with a private investor in 2017.

 To build a long-term, successful enterprise, when you don't close a sale, open a relationship.

Patricia Fripp,
Writer and Speaker

All along, I was trying to improve. Clearly, I was not as good as I thought, or there was something very important I didn't know. So, I started reading. I devoured as many books on sales, leadership, and entrepreneurship as I could get my hands on.

At the same time, I began to observe and make a note of buyers' behavior. The more I read, observed, and noted, the more confused I became. Some things didn't make sense. I'm an engineer, always looking for a logical explanation, even if there isn't one.

We're living in the best times since man was created.

We have the highest ever life expectancy.

We have the highest ever quality of life.

We are richer than ever (as a whole) and yet, unhappier than ever.

We have more material goods than ever before, but we are less satisfied than ever.

There are more suicides in developed countries than anywhere else, and we have the highest number of juvenile suicides ever.

One billion people suffer from depression, a huge percentage of them being in the developed world.

At the same time, we live in a time where, after a single phone call, the food of our choice is delivered to our homes within 30 minutes. With a single click on our computer, we can order everything. Anything, from a ring to a mobile phone, can be ordered with a single click and delivered to our door in a few days. And while all of this is happening, consumer behavior requires psychiatric monitoring. Often, public behavior is not governed by the laws of logic.

So, I exchanged the subject matter of the books I'd been reading for books about consumer psychology and the way the brain works when we buy.

The situation became clearer.

I can't say I liked the conclusions I came to at first. Mostly, however, I was surprised by the buyer's predominant emotion: fear.

Fear?

But why?

PART 1

" Your direction is more important than your speed.

Richard L. Evans

The Ten Commandments

1. Be a patient listener.
2. Never look bored.
3. Wait for the the other person to express their political views and then agree with them.
4. Do the same with religious beliefs.
5. Do not look scruffy.
6. Do not get drunk.
7. Use sexual innuendo, but do not continue unless the other person shows great interest.
8. Do not talk about diseases.
9. Do not violate the privacy of others. They'll tell you everything about themselves eventually anyway.
10. Do not show off. Simply show how important you are in your own way.

When I read these 10 rules, they sounded like the commandments, the 'Moses' of sales took down from the mountain and shared with the global market. But I was wrong.

> **"** I have always said that everyone is in sales. Maybe you don't hold the title of a salesperson, but if the business you are in requires you to deal with people, you, my friend, are in sales.
>
> **Zig Ziglar,**
> Writer and Sales Trainer

The Eiffel Tower was built in 1889 and was the entrance to the World Fair in Paris. It was authorized to stay standing for 20 years after the exhibition, and no one ever imagined it would become the future symbol of Paris.

People reacted fiercely. They considered it a monstrosity. In particular, a group of artists and architects signed a letter to the minister in charge asking him not to allow the construction of 'the useless and monstrous Eiffel Tower' that had nothing to do with the 'hitherto untouched beauty of Paris'.

Consequently, and mainly due to the use of the tower for telecommunications, it was decided that it should remain. People no longer reacted. Paris had gotten used to the ugly monument.

In May 1925, Victor Lustig appeared on the scene with documents and stamps of the Paris Ministry of Post and Telegraphs and sent letters to scrap dealers urgently requesting to see company representatives at the Hôtel de Crillon.

Representatives of the six largest companies attended the meeting, eager to learn what the French Government wanted of them.

After a very expensive meal and plenty of wine, Lustig announced that the city of Paris had finally decided to demolish the Eiffel Tower and sell the material to the highest bidder.

He charismatically told them that for the time being, it was to be kept secret from the residents of Paris.

His intention was to force the companies to bid for the precious contract offered by the French Government. André Poisson, who bid $70,000 (about a million in today's money), was the winner. It was a huge amount, but for Poisson, who was new to the city and wanted to enhance his reputation, it was worth it.

There was, however, a significant problem. Victor Lustig did not work for the government. He was a con artist.

He was born in Austria-Hungary in 1890, and at an early age, decided to travel the world. To finance his adventures, he filched money from naive rich gentlemen whom he met on the transatlantic voyages he undertook at the time. Playing the rich young gentleman, he hosted dinners and receptions to embezzle his associates' money. When the conversation turned to his income, he set the trap.

Requesting absolute confidentiality, he would reveal the 'money box'. It was a magic device that printed money legally and limitlessly. His friends looked in surprise as he inserted a note at one end, turned the crank handle, and retrieved bank notes from the other. Bank notes Lustig would later use these bank notes to pay for his friends' dinner.

What his friends did not know was that the device already contained real money and the note he inserted was simply destroyed.

Jokingly, Lustig would say that it was the only device literally worth its money. People begged Lustig to sell them the device, but he always refused. After much pressure and many offers, of course, he gave in, and began his next journey on the lookout for new victims.

This time, however, he decided to play his biggest trick.

He was going to sell the Eiffel Tower!

After meetings with corporate representatives of the Eiffel Tower, who arrived in limousines he'd provided, Lustig chose his victim. When he met Poisson, he said he was not rich but lived on the salary of a high-ranking civil servant. He handed out contracts on behalf of the French state, demanding complete confidentiality because 'some things should not be told.'

Poisson knew where things were heading. He would have to pay a little extra to secure the contract. The deal was closed at a total of $90,000. The State would take $70,000 and the other $20,000 would go to the intermediate, Mr Lustig.

A few days later, Poisson realized he had been conned but decided not to say anything for fear of making a fool of himself in Parisian society, and to avoid being accused of bribery. Lustig became rich with a clean slate and without a single accusation against him. After several more fraud cases, Lustig was finally arrested and sent to prison. There, he wrote the 'Ten Commandments for Con Men', which are mentioned at the beginning of this chapter.

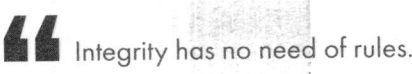 Integrity has no need of rules.

Albert Camus

On July 20, 1969, Neil Armstrong and Buzz Aldrin landed Apollo 11 on the moon.

"One small step for man, one giant leap for mankind."

Prior to this mission, long and arduous preparation had taken place in simulated conditions in a desert in western USA. Indigenous Americans, or Indians, as the rest of the world calls them, still lived in the area.

One day, during training, the two astronauts were approached by an elderly indigenous man, who asked them what they were doing there. When they explained, the elderly man asked a big favor of them:

"We believe that holy spirits live on the moon, so I would like to ask you to convey a message to them from the people of my tribe."

Wishing to satisfy the elderly man's request, the astronauts asked him what the message was. The Indian American asked them to repeat a phrase until they had learned it perfectly. When the astronauts asked what the message meant, he said he couldn't tell them because it was a secret that only the spirits of the moon should hear. When they returned to base, the astronauts looked for someone who could speak the tribe's language. After much effort, they found a university professor. They repeated the message, and the professor couldn't stop laughing. When he'd calmed down, he translated the message.

"Do not believe a word these people say. They came to steal your land."

Why did he say that? Why was he so confident about the ill intent of the mission? Based on the experience of the previous ones, of course. The unfortunate past was to blame. The same applies to sales. You need to build a level of trust starting with a low level of credibility. Maybe that's why start-up founders often say, "I'm not a salesperson."

Judging by movies like *The Wolf of Wall Street,* we can see where this reluctance comes from.

But is this the role model of today's salesperson?

Do you have to be Jordan Belford to sell?

Do you have to grab the customer by the throat to get the product out of your warehouse, as Grand Cardone says?

My answer is no. Clearly not.

So, who are the successful salespeople?

Probably the ones who understand what customers want.

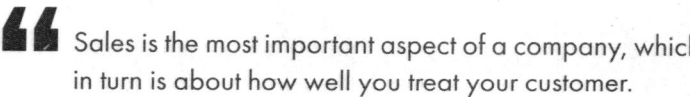 Sales is the most important aspect of a company, which in turn is about how well you treat your customer.

Mark Cuban,
Businessman and Investor

What Do
Customers Want?

Of the 800,000 apps in the App Store in 2013, only 80 had a turnover of more than one million dollars. While applications related to health issues lasted no longer than a few months, an application that simulated the sound of a fart was at the top of the most successful ones.

In 1980, before social media and the Internet, Hoover decided to launch an ad to increase its sales by 4%. The ad said that for every Hoover vacuum cleaner sold in the next 15 days, the buyer will receive two free airline tickets.

They were expecting an increase of four to five percent, but it all went crazy. Customers bought two and even three vacuum cleaners just to get the airline tickets.

As a result, Hoover stopped the campaign two days later. This move, however, caused enormous damage to the brand, resulting in the resignation of the CEO and the Marketing Director.

Reading the story on a website, I thought that this would have gone viral in seconds in the age of social media. Two years ago, United Airlines forcibly removed a passenger from his seat on a plane, despite him having a ticket and a boarding pass. The passenger refused to get up from his seat, claiming he was a physiotherapist and was seeing a client at 8 a.m. the following day. The passenger was punched by a company security officer, and the story was broadcast around the world.

Passengers across the Americas were disgusted by the 'unacceptable company and the callous employees who treated passengers like animals.'

Madness also prevailed on social networks. I was sure United was heading for closure. However, a month later, ticket sales had not fallen, and the share price rose by 10%.

What happened?

Which bit did I not get?

In 1985, Coca Cola introduced the New Coke with a new taste. Millions were spent on the advertising campaign. Coca Cola was on the verge of a great experiment; they were replacing a successful recipe with something new.

The market reaction, however, was frightening. Sales fell

sharply. Consumers of the famous soft drink turned their backs on the new taste, which was sweeter and more like Pepsi. The public was angry. The same night, the main news broadcast was clear:

The Coca Cola company failed to predict the sheer frustration and anger caused by its action. Tens of thousands of people rose up to demand the return of the old recipe.

Coca Cola even opened a call center to take customer complaints, which exceeded 600,000! Of course, the company had done all the necessary market research. In blind trials carried out from 1981 to 1984, 200,000 people chose the new flavor at a rate of 55%. Most of them, in fact, could not distinguish the difference between the two.

In February 2003, British Airways announced that it intended to permanently ground Concorde. Tickets for flights on the specific aircraft quickly sold out, and prices rose to historic highs. On the day British Airways' Concorde took off for the last time, the motorway outside the airport was blocked by thousands of people who stopped to watch the final takeoff. The same people had driven along the same road, oblivious to the historic plane that had flown over their heads every day for the past 30 years. What had changed? Why the sudden interest? Something did not make sense.

So, I started to observe what was going on around me.

A popular espresso company charges €0.45 per capsule. If you filled a Nescafé coffee tin with the contents from each capsule, you would be charged about €55 per tin.

If the customer looked at it this way, they'd think they were being ripped off. But they don't compare it to a tin of Nescafé. They compare it to the coffee they get from Starbucks. In the latter case, buying an espresso machine is an excellent investment.

I also realized that restaurants don't have drink menus. There is a wine list, where after 15 pages of white, rosé, and red wines, there's a dog-eared page with beers and cocktails.

Moreover, there's only one wine list. Food menus are distributed to everyone at the table, but there is only one wine list, and it's given to the person it appears will eventually get the bill. So, one person is asked to decide for the whole group by asking the obvious question, 'red or white?'

I realized that wine is the only drink restaurants can charge as much as they want, and no one will complain. Because no one knows how much a bottle of Château La Fleur costs.

Everyone knows how much a bottle of Dewar's costs, so no one can charge you 10 times more, unless Katy Perry is singing at the restaurant.

Later, I noticed that fine restaurants were getting bad reviews on TripAdvisor. Criticisms they did not deserve. Why? I talked to a psychologist while writing this book to get a more holistic view. He created an image for me.

"It's Champions League night. You want to go to a bar with the guys, drink beers, and eat hot dogs. But it's also your mother-in-law's birthday.

"'We're going out with mother,' your wife announces.

"This generally means you go to a restaurant—a rather more expensive one than you'd have chosen—and pay the bill. And of course, you miss out on watching the game with the guys. So, you already have negative feelings about the restaurant. And when they bring you the wine list, you're already starting to think about what to write on TripAdvisor."

I'm still trying to figure out why it is that to get someone to take all 24 of the white antibiotic pills the box contains, all you have to do is change the color of some of them. We are talking about exactly the same pills.

The user is instructed to take the blue pills only when they have finished the white ones. By doing so, 90% of them complete the treatment.

Moreover, I was amazed by the fact that it took Facebook two and a half years to reach 50 million customers, WhatsApp took 15 months, but Angry Birds took just two weeks.

So, what does the customer actually think?

Why did millions of people download a game where slingshots launch birds at smiling pigs?

Why does a person spend €100,000 on a four-wheeler when they never leave the city center?

Why does a customer spend €5,000 on the latest sound system for their car when they don't even have a radio at home?

Why does an item that's been lingering on the shelf for ages sell out as soon as you announce it'll only be available for two more days?

Why does wine taste better if it's served from a heavier bottle?

Why do people think their cars perform better when they're clean?

Why do airline passengers feel safer if there are no advertisements on the outside of the plane?

Why has Uber been so successful, even in countries where taxi services are of the highest standard?

Why do you think something's 15% cheaper when you make a contactless payment?

Why do pharmaceutical companies try to make neutral-flavored drugs taste worse?

Why do people buy champagne for cats?

Why do people buy lights that fit into the toilet basin?

And, why do painkillers work best if they come in a red box and even better if the company that produces them is a well-known brand?

 People with goals succeed because they know where they're going.

Earl Nightingale,
Author

In this book, I try to give answers to these questions and many more, and finally answer everyone's biggest question:

Should start-up founders become psychologists?

So, I asked this question to the CEO of Trizma Neuro, an applied neuroscience start-up based in Belgrade with clients in more than 20 countries. N.D. is the right person to help me answer the question posed by the title of this chapter.

Instead of using classic research methods (focus groups, questionnaires, etc.), he and his associates set aside the conscious part and with specialist technology, ask the subconscious.

"Marketers," he said, "do not understand people. Our theories, whether philosophical or scientific, about what people are, how they behave, how decisions are made in their brains, what stimulates them, were wrong.

"They were wrong because, until recently, we didn't have the tools to study the human brain.

"Imagine that until 1990 and 2000, we were teaching marketing students about consumer behavior with the black box theory.

"That is, stimuli enter the brain and behavior comes out. You buy or you don't buy. But what happens between the inflow and the outflow? The black box. This can lead to misreading the situation.

"If, for example, I see a child playing basketball from the window of my office, and at the same time, the stock market goes up, I consider it a coincidence. If the same thing happens several times, I consider it a pattern and wait for it to repeat itself. This happens due to two unrelated things.

"This has changed now. In the last 25 years, the MRI and the PET scan have been discovered, as well as encephalography, where we can see what's happening in a matter of seconds.

"Since then, everything has changed because now we can measure it in real time. And do you know what we discovered? The subconscious and conscious mind agree at a rate of about 20%!

"Humans are very bad at reading their own emotions. That's where the encephalogram comes in. So, when we talk about a feeling, we are clearly talking about the subconscious. That is where decisions are made.

"A survey was conducted in London a few years ago. This survey showed that only 2.5% of our behavior depends on attitude research.

"And all the research we do in marketing and business is like that. Do you like this? Don't you like this? Would you go? Wouldn't you go? Would you suggest it? Would you not suggest it?

"The other 97.5% of your behavior is not explained by what you tell me. Logic doesn't pull the strings. Logic is amazing, and we need it."

So, we don't just have to be psychologists; we also have to be neuroscientists!

We should probably start with the basics.

PART 2

&& While you were debating if the glass was half empty or half full, I sold it.

Anonymous

Can You Sell It?

IBM was founded in New York State in 1911. It was co-inventor along with Harvard University of the first machine that could perform complex calculations automatically.

Along the way, it created the first large-scale computer based on vacuum tubes, the first data disc storage system, the first laptop, and much more. It has always been a leading force in the field of technology.

At some point in its long history, it ran into problems that led to low turnover. It then hired McKinsey to diagnose the problem and recommend solutions. The contract was worth three million dollars, a huge amount for that time.

A few months later, McKinsey returned with the result. The problem was 'low sales'.

IBM executives were puzzled . . . three million dollars for that?

"We knew that. What solution do you propose?" they said.

"High sales," was the answer.

So, the sales department hired more people and designed appropriate training. The products were not to blame. Sales just had to increase.

Sometimes, it's as easy as that. As a well-known market executive once said to me, "Companies don't have trouble with expenses. They have trouble with income."

Starting out with Entranet, I took it for granted that I'd have to learn about leadership tactics, rather than sales tactics. And that with an innovative product—the first in the world—sales would inevitably skyrocket, so I would have to be trained in production management. In other words, I devoted my time to everything except what really mattered. Start-up founders usually tick like this.

> *'Who needs sales? If I produce an excellent product that satisfies a need, customers will come flocking on their own.'*

Actually, the question is not whether you can produce it; it's whether you can sell it.

Blendtec is a blender production company. Its story begins in the most typical way. The engineer-owner of the company believed that if he created something exceptional at the right price, sales would skyrocket.

"I always wanted to have the strongest, fastest things. Toys, engines, cars . . . it didn't matter. In 1968, I got married and one of the wedding guests gave us a blender. I thought I could make a better one, so for years, we were developing a blender that would never break.

"We are an engineering business. We have 40 engineers, far more than any other blender company in the world.

"The negative thing was that none of us were salespeople. We assumed that if we made the best blender in the world, customers would be queuing outside the factory gate.

"As soon as someone ordered a fruit juice or a milkshake in a coffee shop, I assumed they would automatically buy one of our blenders. They would ask the employee, literally write down the name of our blender on a piece of paper, and come and buy it.

"I was sure that was how a good product is sold.

"I was mistaken. Tragically mistaken!

"After a while, we decided to hire a salesperson.

"'What's that pile of dust?' the new employee asked one day. They told him it was my way of checking the strength of the blades by putting heavily durable objects in the blender and blending them to dust. He went to the supermarket and bought a six packs of Coca-Cola, some marbles, a chicken, pan handles, and other random items, and brought them to me to put in the blender. We set to work, and he set up a camera to record it. Five days later, he returned.

"'Tom, it's unbelievable. We have six million views on YouTube,' he exclaimed full of excitement.

"That was the beginning of the series, 'Will it blend?', which currently lists 145 videos and 500 million views.

"And that's how sales began!"

 My biggest mistake in my first year as an entrepreneur was that I tried to be much too of a business owner when instead, I should have learned how to sell first.

Patrick Bet-David,
Businessman

We are all salespeople. Whether you're selling yourself to an employer, your product to customers, your start-up to investors, or your idea to your employees and partners, at the end of the day, we all are selling something. You can design the best product that meets a genuine consumer need at a great price. But if you can't sell it, your start-up closes down. And that's the end of it.

That's why selling is probably the most important part of implementing your idea. Because if it doesn't go well, you're left with the bitter taste of defeat.

In 1811, Isaac Singer, the son of Germa-Jewish immigrants, was born in New York. Growing up in poverty, young Isaac dreamt of becoming an actor. He left home at a young age and started performing with a theater company. The tour, however, was not deemed successful and the aspiring actor had to earn his living by other means.

Being good with his hands, he began to design and build machines. He built a machine that drilled holes in rocks, and soon after, a printer.

But none of his machines sold as expected and in 1850, he was living in a basement, poor and hungry. That basement, however, would change his life.

The owner of the basement made sewing machines, which often broke down, and he would bring them to Singer to have them repaired.

Singer quickly realized he could make much better machines than those on the market. So, he took out a loan and in 11 days, his first sewing machine was ready. It was sold immediately.

In 1863, 20,000 sewing machines were sold, making Singer rich. So much so that the parties held at his mansion were social events and always made it to the newspapers of the time. He was living the life of a tycoon. He had countless female companions and children scattered throughout America. And all this just a few years after the basement and the misery.

How did he do it?

Singer was a charismatic salesman. He was also way ahead of his time in promoting his sewing machines. He hired experienced tailors to use his machines in department store windows. Being very theatrical himself, he would hold presentations anywhere that gathered an audience. Be it performances, circuses, festivals, and social events, he'd always be there.

People loved to watch his unique presentation of sewing machines. Venues filled to see Singer perform. At the end of the 19th century, the Singer Company sold 80% of all sewing machines in America.

We live in the age of the new; the age of innovation. Some years ago, a survey revealed that the most common word in advertising in the previous century was not buy, cheap or warranty.

It was the word *new*. But the truth is, we don't like innovation.

According to a very popular (among psychologists) psychological phenomenon called the 'mere-exposure effect', people tend to develop a preference for certain things simply because they are familiar with them. In social psychology, this phenomenon is sometimes referred to as the 'principle of familiarity'.

Why do we like old songs and their cover versions so much?

Why were the most popular films in previous decades either sequels or remakes of older ones?

The answer is *familiarity*.

The well-known music platform Spotify developed an application called Discover Weekly. Using this application, Spotify sent 30 new songs every Monday to your mobile phone by artists you had never heard before, which were selected according to your general music preferences. The algorithm, however, had a glitch; an incorrect function that sent the user older, familiar songs along with the new, unheard ones. They realized quickly and fixed the problem. They also discovered that as soon as they fixed the problem, use of the application collapsed. The bottom line was that by adding familiar songs to the new ones, users responded much better.

This was the application's recipe for success.

But here, we're talking about start-ups. Usually, these types of companies combine innovation and opportunity. We're presenting something new, something innovative, something maybe ahead of its time, which at the same time, should be familiar. How is this going to work?

Raymond Loewy was one of the most famous industrial designers of the 20th century.

He was born in Paris in the late 19th century, but designed almost everything from Lucky Strike cigarettes to America's most popular car of the 20th century, the Studebaker. His signature design appeared on trains, buses, tractors and the Air Force 1, the aircraft of the American president.

Rayon Loewy believed that to sell a product, you had to follow the MAYA theory—Most Advanced Yet Acceptable. In other words, 'very sophisticated but at the same time acceptable'.

He believed that man needs novelty and innovation, but on the other hand, there is also the fear of 'something new'. A deep conservatism that, to go beyond product design, needed to border between neophilia and neophobia. He claimed that to sell something familiar, you have to make it unexpected, but at the same time, to sell something unexpected, you have to make it familiar.

On August 26, 1940, Don Lafontaine was born in Duluth, Minnesota.

At the age of 13, his voice broke literally in the middle of a sentence. The next day at school, he was ashamed to speak. When his friends heard him, they were thrilled. Finally, they had found someone to call the school principal and say:

"My son is ill. He can't come to school today."

Don Lafontaine is the man who has lent his voice to more than 5,000 Hollywood movie trailers, hundreds of thousands of commercials, internet videos, and even online games. His voice is linked with the phrase 'in a world'.

Among thousands, Don and four other professionals in the field are the ones who made millions.

Why?

Because whoever hears his voice knows that the soon-to-be-released film will be another great success, just like others they have seen. They link the voice to the movie.

They are certain that behind this voice is a hidden group that makes successful hits, even if this isn't true.

This is how you can link your product to a large number of customers: by constantly and consistently repeating the message.

So, if you want someone to trust you, you have to tell them the same story over and over again. Persistence is what counts the most.

When the consumer acknowledges and connects it to a brand, the familiarity will undoubtedly become trust. And if you gain their trust, the sale becomes much easier.

❝ You can have everything in life you want if you will just help other people get what they want.

Zig Ziglar,
Writer and Sales Trainer

The Easiest Ways to Sell

Sales are about people. According to Sandler, the easiest sale is achieved when your product is aimed at someone who is in 'pain' and wants to deal with it right now.

The second easiest way is by referring to a 'pain' they'll face in the future. The third is the 'pain' they may confront in the future and want to be prepared for, and the fourth is linked to a desire. This applies to all products and companies around the world.

However, you have a product—innovative, no doubt—that seeks to meet a need currently met by the competition, usually by a well-known company with a registered name and track record. Or a need that the potential customer doesn't even know he has, in which case, your situation is different.

> ❝ Approach each customer with the idea of helping him or her to solve a problem or achieving a goal, not selling a product or service.
>
> **Brian Tracy,**
> Writer and Sales Trainer

I believe that there are three easiest ways to sell:

First. Have something a person really needs.

Frank Sinatra was born in 1915 in New Jersey. At the age of 16, he dropped out of school and had a series of jobs, such as dockworker and newsboy. However, he quickly got bored and quit each job after just a few weeks. When he finally quit his job of installing refrigeration units on cargo ships, his father had had enough. He called him a 'quitter'.

"If you want to be a bum, go somewhere else and be a bum," he said.

He didn't have to tell him again. Frank packed his bags and took a train to New York. His goal was to become a singer. But doors didn't open for the skinny Italian. He couldn't find work as a singer in any of the clubs. With no place to stay and no money for food, he returned home.

Apparently, Dolly made fun of her son's ambitions. She called him Mr Singer but secretly started visiting clubs asking the owners to give her son a chance. It resulted very quickly in him being invited to perform at the Hoboken Club. But the job didn't last long. Frank got into a fight with the owner, who kicked him out. When Frank was 17, his parents lent him $65 to buy a portable address book and a binder to arrange his sheet music. This put him a step ahead of other aspiring artists looking for jobs in the clubs. Frank began a collection of musical arrangements. He later explained his strategy.

"The bands needed them. I had them. If a local band wanted to use my archive (and they always did because I had a large collection readily available) they had to agree to take on Sinatra as the singer."

Frank was able to establish himself on the local scene and eventually conquer globally.

 People buy what they want; not what they need.

Daniel Priestley,
Speaker and Best-selling Author

Second. Have something the customer wants.

On November 20, 1945, the Nuremberg trials began. Leading figures of the Nazi movement as well as many lower-ranking officials were up in court. Among them were the war criminals of the concentration camps who survived being lynched after the arrival of the allied troops.

On the other side of the globe was a concentration camp in Japanese-occupied Manchuria that inflicted enormous atrocities on Chinese and American captives making Auschwitz look like an amusement park.

An army of Japanese scientists, some say as many as 3,000, conducted inhuman experiments until the end of the war. Not a single victim escaped the brutality of this camp. The unit consumed eight tons of tetanus and cholera bacteria per month. They injected germs into the ankles and tongues of the captives and observed their reactions. They cut the infected limbs to see if the infection would grow and how the victim reacted. They gave them hydrocyanic acid and watched the 'guinea pigs' die while freezing the victims to very low temperatures to observe the spread of the disease.

There was always a supply of 70 to 80 prisoners so the experiments could continue. Unit 731 caused tens of thousands of deaths and an outbreak of the plague in 1942 caused by contaminated grains and rice dropped from aeroplanes in China.

After the end of the war, the 3,000 scientists returned home. They were known to the allied forces.

Why were they not punished?

Why weren't they treated the same as the Nazi 'scientists'?

The disbanded Unit 731 commissioned Japanese Colonel Ryoichi Naito to negotiate with his American counterpart, Colonel Murray Saunders. The Americans wanted the results of the research and the Japanese wanted amnesty. An agreement was reached fearing that if the public found out about Unit 731, there would be a nightmare. They all kept their mouths shut.

The worst part of the story came when a later investigation of the scientists discovered that one of them was the owner of a large hematological clinic in Osaka, another was the secretary of the Japanese Penicillin Association, and a third was honored with the Grand Cordon of the Order of Rising Sun for his scientific contribution.

 Best way to sell something: don't sell anything. Earn awareness, respect and trust of those who might buy.

Jordan Belfort,
The Wolf of Wall Street

Third. Have something your customers' customers want.

In 1897, chemist Felix Hoffmann, who was working for the small drug company Bayer, discovered aspirin. He discovered it while trying to help his father, who was in severe pain caused by rheumatoid arthritis. Hoffmann Senior had been taking salicylic acid until then.

The side effects, however, were very strong. The chemist decided to make its administration more tolerable.

At the time, the substance no longer needed to be taken from plants and could be produced in a lab.

When he realized his father was feeling and functioning much better than before with this medication, he took it to his manager at Bayer. His manager rejected the product as useless and possibly dangerous.

The real reason, however, was different. At the time, Bayer had launched a new cough syrup. A magical product that gave a sense of euphoria to those who took it. Ordinary workers were turned into heroes. That's why it was called heroin. Of course, no one was interested in the side effects back then. So, Hoffmann's general manager was not interested in aspirin.

Hoffmann did not hold back. He took his discovery to a hospital in Berlin and recognition of the drug came from the patients themselves.

It was then that Bayer's general manager realized that he had made a mistake. He patented the aspirin himself, on behalf of his company, and the small drug company grew into the giant we know today.

So, if you have a big new idea that potential customers approve of, but investors reject, don't be disappointed. Remember that even aspirin went through this phase before it went into production.

Sales is not about selling anymore, but about building trust and educating.

Siva Devaki,
CEO of Mass Mailer

Trust

CBS is one of the most popular media stations in America. The channel's news programme enjoyed the highest viewing rates in the 1960s and 1970s. Walter Cronkite, a news presenter for 19 consecutive years from 1962 to 1981 can be thanked for this.

In 1970, a poll was conducted among Americans about which public figure American citizens trusted most, and Walter Cronkite came out on top by a wide margin.

Next on the list were the President of the United States and religious leaders, followed by members of the Senate, Congress, etc. This, of course, had not developed overnight. It took many years of continuous presence and consistency of word and deed for the legendary American journalist to build such a profile.

Simon Sinec says, "Developing trust is like developing muscle. Like going to a gym. On the first day, you'll see nothing. On the second day, you may feel some pain. If, however, you continue to go, in two weeks, you'll begin to see results. After two months, you realize that your effort achieved results and you start developing muscle."

This means perseverance, patience, and consistency are required, but it is also important to constantly get the message across; the right message—the message that expresses you.

> **"** Remember, people don't believe it when we say it, they believe it when they say it.
>
> **Shari Levitin,**
> Author and Speaker

Research shows that a company's performance is judged by its relationships with customers.

But what determines the creation of these relationships?

What is the number one factor that influences these relationships?

All studies indicate the trust factor.

But what is trust?

Trust is the choice to let go, take risks, and appear vulnerable to the other side.

Which companies enjoy the highest level of customer trust?

Entrepreneur.com lists companies such as Nike, Coca Cola, Amazon, Apple, and Southwest Airlines.

Why? How do you know that when you leave your suitcases with Southwest Airlines you won't lose them? How do you know that when you drink Coca Cola or a coffee at Starbucks you won't get ill?

The iTunes' Terms of Use Agreement is 229 pages long. I don't know a single person who has read it. But everyone signs it. Why?

Because you trust the company. Because you've done it before without consequences. Because millions of others did the same before and nothing happened to them. Because these companies are made up of people who know what they're doing, so you trust their capability.

Even with the best product at the best price, if there is a lack of trust, the effort fails.

Two English comedians carried out a bold experiment. They asked Ed Sheeran, one of the most popular singers in the world, to play in the basement of a building on a notorious street. They put up signs outside the shop and a badly dressed guy invited passersby to come in to see Ed Sheeran perform for just £2.

Two and a half hours later, no one agreed to it. The day ended after taking just £4 from a daring couple of tourists, who could not believe their luck. It's not every day you get a private concert from a world-famous singer.

The street salesperson did what the salesman's manual said. He spoke to people promoting his product, chose a different strategy for each potential customer that passed by and even created a sense of urgency, saying that Ed Sheeran would only be there until noon.

But nothing was able to overcome the lack of trust the situation created, even if the salesperson was telling the truth. That, if nothing else, was especially appealing.

Why? Because 'what's the worst thing that can happen?' is the consumer's main concern.

If the outcome is likely to be awful, that's all a person can think of.

So, you have a product that has been seen barely on the market before, or the customer you are going to sell it to is not familiar with it at all. You can't rely on the privilege of trust because you have no track record. You're a young person trying to convince a high-ranking executive, who will take a risk by trusting you.

So, to make a sale, you have to gain their trust. They know neither what you are about to recommend nor how much of their time you are going to waste.

They certainly don't want to jeopardize the company's capital on something that poses a great risk to themselves and their associates. And they certainly don't want to invest time and money in a bad choice.

The only reason they're giving you a chance is to feel better. They want to solve a real issue in order to make their life easier.

The only way it can be done is to trust you. Otherwise, they're risking more than they're willing to lose. And it's not just about money. It's about their position in the company, the ability to make the right decisions, and the distrust a wrong decision could bring to their name. So obviously, they'll have to trust you.

According to Frances Frei, a Harvard professor, there are three basic rules of trust:

1. The customer feels you know what you're talking about and you're capable of doing what you say.
2. They sense you're being authentic.
3. If they feel you understand their needs and will do everything necessary for them, you have a better chance of being trusted.

When these three rules work simultaneously, your chances of closing a deal with the person sitting across the table are greatly increased.

The third rule is more easily challenged, of course. You are there to sell, to meet your own needs, not the customer's.

So, how would the potential client sense that his interests are your first priority?

You take time to listen and understand the need. To provide a solution customized to the consumer's needs. But who has the time to develop the complete understanding and connection between the two parties to close the deal?

Usually, neither of them.

So, it is up to you to prove in a very short time that you are an 'expert' on the client's business and convince them you can provide a solution.

How do you do that?

Ask and listen. Do not talk! Listen.

Try to understand the problem by putting yourself in the other person's shoes. Ask if what you would do makes sense, or if more information is required to understand other aspects of your client's business.

First, you need to find the problem that needs a solution. Then find out where you can help.

At the same time, the client needs to understand the problems the situation causes in their everyday life.

You must persevere until they spell out the problems causing that situation and what it would be like afterwards if you were to find a solution.

They must also understand what the problem is costing the company. In terms of labor, attitude, and money.

Continue with questions.

How do you see a solution to the problem? How would you solve it if you could? What do you think your life would be like afterwards? By making the client think creatively about their problem, they will recognize the parameters better and concentrate on the need to find a solution. At the same time, you can help them with questions such as:

We dealt with this issue in another field and successfully resolved it by . . .

- How would you feel about doing something similar in your situation?
- Where do you see opportunities for improvement?
- How long has this been troubling you?
- How long have you been wanting to resolve it?
- What would be the ideal way to solve the problem?
- How can I help you?

All things being equal, people will do business with a friend; all things being unequal, people will still do business with a friend.

Mark McCormack,
Author

Authenticity.

Now, human instinct is working against you. People can easily tell if you are being authentic or not. The easiest solution is, of course, to be yourself. But what if your real self is not good enough for the other person? What if you give the wrong impression?

Usually, personal choices and insecurities lead us to hide things and details about our real selves. That's when we are not authentic.

On the other hand, a person will trust you when you have things in common. When they think you remind them of themselves. Obviously, we trust ourselves because we know ourselves better than anyone else. But what if you are different? The answer is not to hide things but to reveal them. Show who you really are. Good people—the people you would like to work with—will appreciate it!

Returning to the value that knowledge of the market has, I would like to tell you a story.

As a young man and a new salesman in a company, I attended a sales seminar. Entering the room, the trainer left an envelope on his desk and said, "'Today, you are selling horses.' So, someone comes into the store and tells you he wants a horse. Sell it.

"One by one, we took the floor and started making arguments. I have a good horse, a fast horse, a beautiful horse, an Arabic, a racehorse, white, black, red, tall, strong, and anything else you can think of. We all related what we had and what we could offer. Nobody asked what the customer wanted.

"The trainer opened the envelope and read the letter inside. It turned out that the client wanted a horse for a blind friend, who had a horse for many years and had recently died.

"We were selling him black and white racehorses when a lame horse would have suited his need. All the customer needed was the presence of a horse to be happy.

"In short, you need to understand the real extra value for the customer and then offer it to him."

What differentiates sellers today is their ability to bring fresh ideas.

Jill Konrath,
Writer and Speaker

Consultant, Not Salesperson

In 1972, *The Godfather* was released, a cinematic masterpiece by Francis Ford Coppola. Marlon Brando, in the role of the Godfather, won both the Golden Globe and the Oscar for leading male actor.

For the uninitiated, the story takes place in New York in 1945. The 'elite' of the underworld and prominent members of American society attend Don Vito Corleone's daughter's wedding. (Any similarity to the reality of the time is deemed inaccurate and not the author's intention.)

Don Vito's third son Michael (Al Pacino) is an idealistic and intelligent young man who volunteered for the Marines in World War II, despite his family's disagreement, and stood out for his bravery. He had just been demobilized from the army and planned to complete his education. He dreams of a normal, legal life despite his father's ambitions.

After many developments as well as bullets, Don Corleone ends up in hospital with multiple injuries but survives.

Despite his original plan, Michael is forced to enter the game. He takes over the reins of the family and the role of the Godfather.

In an unforgettable scene, Marlon Brando tells Al Pacino: "Soon, Emilio Barzini (head of a similar family, inspired by the Genoa criminal family in New York) will request a meeting. He will do it via someone you trust completely, who will guarantee your safety. In this meeting, they will kill you."

He continued talking about wine, family, and the weather. Shortly, before they go their separate ways, he returns to the subject.

"Now, listen . . . whoever comes to the meeting with Barzini is the traitor. Do not forget that!"

Absolute knowledge of the subject! Certainty about how things will turn out, to the extent that life will be lost once the described situation occurs. No room for second thoughts, or uncertainty.

"Whoever tells you about the meeting is the traitor. And at this meeting, you'll be killed. Be prepared."

If only there was someone to tell us with absolute confidence what to do in any situation. A consultant to elaborate that wherever you go, that particular group of investors wants to hear about your company's growth plan. So, spend more time on foreign market expansion than on cost analysis.

A mentor who can predict that a specific idea has a 55% chance of success and will rise by 20% if you make certain moves.

We're all looking for a consultant with the ultimate knowledge, if only on a very limited subject.

So, when we eventually find that person, every piece of their advice will be invaluable.

 Stop selling, start helping.

Zig Ziglar,
Writer and Sales Trainer

An up-and-coming business executive decides to gift himself a tailor-made suit for his business meetings instead of buying one off the rail.

So, he invites a tailor recommended by a friend to his office. The tailor begins with relaxed questions, showing him color charts and fabric samples while informing the customer about fashion trends and the usefulness of various options at the same time.

They conclude that the customer wants a business suit that won't crease easily when traveling by plane, with two or three buttons and specific pockets. The tailor then suggests he choose a specific cut, so the shoulders don't puff up when he sits down opposite his business partner and impress with a quality outfit.

He also came up with the following alternatives:

"First of all, there's a fabric combination of mohair, silk, and cashmere. We call it 'Elton John' because of its superb quality but also very high price."

The executive first thought it sounded too expensive for the money he was willing to spend.

"The simplest and most economical option is the one we call 'low-level executive', which consists of . . ."

That's where the customer stopped listening. He was not a low-ranking executive, and therefore, not interested in that option.

He was left with the intermediate option—the option the salesman wanted to offer the customer from the start. Before closing the deal, the salesman continued with some questions.

"Would you like one vent or two at the back?"

He replied that one would probably be better.

"To be totally honest, if you have one vent and you're used to putting your hands in your pockets, when the closed part of the jacket separates, a large area at the back of your trousers will be exposed. This may not be an image you want to convey.

On the other hand, if you have two vents, when you put your hands in your pockets, the jacket falls evenly, keeping your image from the back intact."

The deal was done. The consultant knew his subject and the customer knew he had made the right choice.

You will attract way more buyers if you are offering to teach them something of value than you will ever attract by simply trying to sell them your product.

Chet Holmes,
Writer and Film Producer

Impartial advice creates the feeling that customers are dealing with friends.

Southwest Airlines agents are trained to show they really care about the passenger. For example, when a customer called to ask for a ticket from Dallas to Rhode Island, the search came up with a complicated route with expensive fares and two transfers. The Southwest employee then said,

"I could never put you through such inconvenience.

Give me a minute to look for alternatives."

In a matter of seconds, the agent came up with two direct routes at a reasonable cost with other airlines. In fact, she went a step further and suggested the company she would choose. The customer had no reason not to trust Southwest now.

And talking about the other side of the Atlantic, I'll share a personal experience. On May 22, 2016, I departed for America. I arrived in Miami the same night and got ready for a tour like any of the great artists who perform abroad. Five cities in six days, in three states. Fort Lauderdale, Denver, Los Angeles, San Diego, Orlando and back to Miami for the return flight on Saturday, May 28. Time was short. I prepared for my next meetings on the flights.

One afternoon, just before I got to the hotel, I went to a supermarket to buy some groceries. At the fruit counter, I heard a saleswoman asking a customer a question.

"I see you got two pounds of apples. Would you like me to give you a recipe for apple pie free of charge?"

The customer thanked her politely and said she was indeed going to make an apple pie but already had a magic recipe from her grandmother that she dutifully follows every time for the same amazing result.

"Perfect," the saleswoman said.

"If you already have a recipe, maybe you'd like to add a few berries this time. They add to the taste and they're in season now. They're so fresh! Here, try one . . . but just one thing,"

she continued.

"Next time, please come and find me. I'm dying to find out what your children and grandchildren thought, and I have the best recipes for desserts and pies in the whole of California, you know!"

I have never seen a better sale in a grocery store. With a little effort, the saleswoman sold something of minimal value and gained a loyal customer.

For sure, the next time the customer goes to the store, she'll ask for the same employee. Apart from the familiarity, she has something else to gain, and something more to learn.

The same happens with start-ups. The market gives you a thirst for learning: new trends, technological developments, new ways of approaching customers, but also what the competition has in mind. What's more, the market is interested in learning how to solve today's problems as well as those of the future.

Once you find the answers, you can claim to be selling something that could either get your customer ahead of the competition, or be their accomplice and help them stay in the game, despite the global changes ahead. This is how you can act as a consultant for your client and educate them at the same time.

 If you don't believe in what you're selling, neither will your prospect.

Frank Bettger,
Author

Let's go back to 2005. The Greeks are living the dream. Just a year before, Greece was in the global spotlight, having successfully organized the best Olympic Games in history, won the Eurovision Song Contest, and after the alignment of all the planets, the Euro Football Championship 2004.

Construction continues at a steady pace. Banks are still lending money to everyone and borrowers as the recipients are keen to renovate their homes.

One day in May, I found myself in an apartment to measure up and bid for a renovation project. The owner, looking forward to a good price, informed me that he has already spoken to five engineers and was awaiting offers.

I continued unperturbed, recording spatial requirements and noting construction details.

Just before I left, I said to the owner, "I'll send you the offer tomorrow afternoon. I'd like to inform you that whoever you decide to work with, you should be very cautious when changing the door and window frames.

"Your house is on the top floor, and I'm almost certain there is no thermal insulation on the roof.

"You do not have mold yet, because your window frames are old. Condensation does not build up inside the house because your windows are not airtight.

"With the new window frames, this will be a problem. Next winter, you'll see mold on the walls. You'll call various builders to waterproof your roof because you think the damp came through the roof. It won't solve the problem, but you'll think the trapped condensation will dry out in the summer. Next winter, the problem will continue, and you'll call in another five engineers to see what to do. By then, you'll be tired of paying for construction work, and you'll look back at the time when there were no problems, even if you spent more on heating. So, what I'm trying to say is that when you change the window frames, you'll also have to insulate the roof. I can recommend some good professionals for the job whether we work together or not."

Then, I left.

I got the job half an hour after I sent the offer. I got it only because I acted as a technical consultant and not a salesman.

People don't care how much you know until they know how much you care.

Theodore Roosevelt,
Former President of the United States

Where Does the Customer Hurt?

Think of yourself as Sherlock Holmes. You are called to solve a crime. Without questions, you decide that the butler is the murderer. The murders continue and you arrest the maid. After putting the fifth wrong person in jail, your coworkers tell you that it's time to quit.

"He's not fit for the job."

Of course, if the butler was the killer, you'd have other problems to deal with. Problems you'll encounter as a start-up.

If you develop a product without researching the market and customer needs, one thing is certain: your lack of knowledge will become obvious when you need to modify your product or upgrade it to meet other needs.

If this happens, you'll likely test your client's patience by risking various approaches, which will probably annoy them without providing a solution. There is no need for that. The process is simple and hasn't changed since ancient times.

Ask, listen, and then provide a solution!

According to Warren Berger, our brains are hungry for information from the moment we're born, with some 40,000 questions being asked between the ages of two and five years.

However, the rate of questions peaks at the age of five and fluctuates immediately thereafter. Children between the ages of five and 12 ask up to 80 questions a day. In middle school, it's 35 to 40. By the time they reach executive age, questions are limited to an average of 50.

The reason for this is the anti-research culture we have developed at home, in schools, and the workplace. Instead of encouraging the questioning process as one of the most natural ways for our brains to learn, we have eliminated it.

In one of the best sales seminars I have ever attended, the speaker was a salesman. He had worked for various companies and, at the time, held the position of sales manager for a wholesale drugs company.

The aim of the company he worked for was to achieve a sales increase of 10% for the current year.

The sales team got together and began to make proposals. The implementation of a large advertising campaign in print and sector magazines was mentioned.

The organization of conferences for pharmacists and their spouses in five-star hotels was also suggested. Nobody thought to ask the pharmacists what they would like.

The next day, after a few phone calls and meetings, the salesman made a decision. He would hire another motorbike delivery employee to deliver medications in the evenings.

With minimal cost, the increased turnover was achieved, and customers were happier than ever.

 If you want to win in life, first learn how to listen.

Dōn Yves

In 1985, Nick Andrews decided to continue his studies at Harvard. Moving from England to the US is not a simple matter, even if the language is the same. Nick, however, had an aunt, who lived alone in Massachusetts for many years.

One night, the phone in his room at the Harvard dorm rang and he was told that his aunt had died a few hours earlier. He went to the hospital to identify the body thinking about the arrangements for the burial he would have to make himself due to the absence of local relatives.

In the pre-internet era, he did what everyone else would have done—he opened the phone book and started taking offers from local funeral homes. The first four mentioned the 'deals', costs, and advantages of each deal.

By the fifth phone call, the situation was different. On the other end of the line was a gentleman who, after asking some exploratory questions, asked, "Could I ask you some personal questions? I can tell by your accent you're not from America. In that case, was your aunt also an English citizen?

"A rather painful and time-consuming bureaucratic process accompanies the death of a foreigner in the United States, you know. Whoever you work with, it would be a good idea to start the process now to avoid any delays later.

"Would you like me to send you the forms to save you the trouble?"

The deal was done because the salesman showed genuine interest by asking a few targeted questions.

It's very important to understand that asking means winning.

Ask questions. As many as you can.

By doing so, you'll clarify whether your product can provide a solution and the customer will realize that, besides a sale, you want to understand. They will analyze the problem and the issues it creates in the daily running of the company, but also their role in it, which is to your advantage.

Sandler's very successful method insists that you need to go even deeper. Don't just focus on the 'pain' but understand the way the business operates, too.

- Who are your customers?
- Who are your best customers?

- How do you find new customers?
- What tools do you use?
- What are the three biggest problems in your industry?
- How long have you been at the company?
- How did you start?
- What are your goals for the company?
- What are your personal goals?
- What are the criteria for choosing a supplier like us?
- What are your goals for the next three years?
- What do you think would go against your goals?
- Are there any opportunities that could be developed?
- Are there any we could implement together?
- What could we do for each other to move forward?

During this questioning process, you can help your prospect by saying something such as:

"We came across something similar in another industry and solved it the following way. Do you think that could help?"

Or

"In another company, we noticed . . . (what you can solve with your product). Have you noticed that too?"

According to Brian Tracy, the right salespeople are the ones who ask the right questions. The highly experienced executive trainer says, "Listen first. Don't start reciting a poem. Do not respond straightaway when they have finished. Wait a while. Pause; otherwise, it will appear you weren't listening, just waiting to speak. Think about what the other person said and then ask.

"After they have spoken, the best questions to get them to continue for more information are 'How do you mean?' and 'what exactly do you mean by this?'

"If you understand what the other person is saying, you'll get to the real problem. Then, you move on to the next level and say, 'Fine. I asked these questions to find out if our product fits your needs. Could you spare a few minutes for me to present it to you?'"

> Seek first to understand then to be understood. This is the basis of good communication.

Stephen Covey,
Author

Dropbox was founded in 2007. At the time of writing, its value has exceeded $10 billion, and has 500 million subscribers and 1,500 employees. It wasn't always that rosy. At some point, they introduced two new products to the market, Mailbox and Carousel. They were expecting similar success to that of their main product, but it never came. After a short time, executives at Dropbox were forced to withdraw the products from circulation. The reasons for failure are common and well-known.

As Dropbox CTO Aditya Agarwal said, "We didn't seek feedback from the customers we were targeting. We created without listening."

Agarwal added, "This was our most painful experience. At the same time, of course, it was the most intuitive and important. It showed us what we were doing wrong when creating new products. We accepted our defeat and carried on better and stronger."

" Do not assume that you are so interesting that you can prevail with chatter and still get away with it.

Mike Greene,
Author

In 2018, Entranet in collaboration with CERTH, the largest research center in Greece, submitted a proposal to the EU to finance the creation of a digital nurse, which would interact with both patients and nursing staff. The proposal was approved a few months later and the group started working on the project.

The problem as far as we could see was clear.

In hospitals and nursing homes, there were folders full of documents at the foot of patients' beds. Time was wasted looking for each patient's schedule or diet. Staff had to refer to the file for all kinds of information. Also, the doctor was always accompanied by other younger doctors who kept notes for each case.

For us, it was obvious that the matter required digital help. A digital nurse, when asked for information, would provide it on a screen next to the patient's bed, and would take any notes needed. The same device would provide the patient with entertainment, information, the operation of 'smart room' devices, and even communication with family and friends by video conferencing as often as they liked.

As we proceeded with the design of the product, I was approached by a Greek student in the second year of the Entrepreneurial Engineering graduate program at the University of Aalborg in Denmark.

He said he was looking for a subject topic for an assignment related to the business development of an existing business product. We decided to collaborate, and he would carry out the market research for digital nursing. For this assignment, Bill interviewed doctors, nurses and administrative staff in hospitals, clinics, nursing homes, and rehabilitation centers, both in the private and the public sector in Greece, Denmark, and the UK.

These interviews gave us a different perspective. Caregivers in nursing homes had very different needs from those we'd imagined. They were afraid to go into rooms at night due to overly 'hospitable' elderly people. They wanted to be able to call for help if the need arose.

In rehabilitation centers, the staff did not want patients to have access to the daily schedule because, in event of a delay, there were endless complaints. Realistically speaking, however, the schedule could not be followed religiously in such centers due to the specifics of the accidents needing to be remedied.

The problem that needed to be solved was different to what we were focusing on. The needs were recorded, the design adapted, and the development continued with far more accurate orientation.

> **"** If you know the enemy and know yourself, you need not fear the result of a hundred battles. If you know yourself but not the enemy, for every victory gained you will also suffer a defeat. If you know neither the enemy nor yourself, you will succumb in every battle.

Sun Tzu,
The Art of War

Know Your Product and the Competition

In 1990, Paramount Home Entertainment, the British distribution company of the TV series *Star Trek*, commissioned a well-known company to promote the 26 episodes that would hit the market that year. To do this, extensive staff training in Star Trek culture, history, and language was required.

More specifically, the marketing director of the company organized a seminar that analyzed all the information and detail the team responsible for the project should know; from the genealogy of the aliens to how radiation works. He explained, "Our product is complex, and our customers are smart. If we make a mistake with a name or use the wrong spaceship, it will undermine the overall credibility of the format and the films themselves."

The same is relevant everywhere. You need to know the subject you are dealing with extremely well.

In 2004, I accepted an offer from a good friend, Aris. His family owned a factory that produced food packaging materials and he was ready to start a business of his own. As in many family businesses, cohabiting generations could not coexist as far as ideas and decisions were concerned.

Aris wanted to deal with a new type of packaging that had appeared in the Balkan countries for the first time, and it looked as if it could gain a large share of the market. It involved the colored polystyrene trays used by most fresh meat businesses today. He proposed I took on a role in the business with an 18% share.

My job seemed cut out. It would be trade-based, in the beginning at least, and the first customers could be drawn from the factory's existing clientele.

I accepted and started the job while continuing with my other businesses. The first foreign contacts were made, and we signed a representation agreement with a packaging company from England. Soon, we expanded and signed contacts with poultry farms and fresh meat packaging companies. Later, we sold the first batch to the largest poultry trading company in Greece.

Along the way, however, I realized that things were much harder than I thought. Some companies had to change their packaging machines to use our products and others had to change their storage system. I had to answer questions and provide solutions in a sector I was unfamiliar with. I was clearly out of my depth.

In my ignorance, I didn't realize that even Aris knew nothing about it. In a family business, such matters were covered up. But when everyone is expecting you to make decisions, it's obvious whether the king is naked or not. And, in this case, he was as naked as it gets.

The adventure ended in 2007 at a huge financial loss for me, being the biggest failure in my professional career.

 If you don't take care of your customer, your competitor will.

Bob Hooey,
Writer and Speaker

While writing this book, I talked to a friend who is a salesman in the construction industry.

In 2014, three competing companies submitted bids for a large shopping center in the Black Sea in Bulgaria. The interested companies had to prove their materials would endure the local conditions. So, each company sent samples.

It would take a month to test the samples to prove their durability. The employer company summoned the three companies again after a month. The sample materials were examined, and one company clearly missed the target and withdrew.

"Just the two of us now," my friend said.

I submitted the specifications of our product as did our competitor. Then I observed the space. Observation is a great quality for a salesperson. I saw a drill on the shelf. I took the tool and drilled a hole in the sample tank. The water ran out and the customer complained that I ruined his tank. I asked him to be patient. I took a bucket from the car and one of our products, and prepared a sample. I filled in the hole and insulated it for 25 seconds. The customer liked what he saw. I knew, for a fact, that my competitor did not have similar materials. In a desperate attempt to spoil things and confuse the customer, he tried to perform a similar experiment using our materials. The game was over. I took an order worth €80,000. The owner informed his engineers, and we started working. This happened because I wasn't just familiar with our products, but with those of the competitors as well. I had taken the necessary time and required effort to stay informed.

In September 2017, the citizens of Santa Monica, California, USA, woke up to see the roads full of abandoned electric scooters. In the days that followed, the news bulletins and morning shows reported on this new trend.

The first company to introduce them was Bird. Bird very quickly became a 'unicorn' (it is a company that reaches a capital value of one billion). It became a unicorn faster than Uber, Airbnb, and Facebook. To be precise, it achieved this surplus value faster than any other company in history.

In the year after its inception, Bird reached two billion dollars. And bear in mind, it's not even the only such company in the marketplace. Other companies started at the same time with exactly the same product. Spin, Lime, Jump, and many more claim the same market share. At the same time, Google, Uber, and Lyft had already invested many millions in these companies.

How did Bird manage to find investor capital in this particular case and from such large companies?

The founder of Bird had previously worked at Uber and Lyft. There were many similarities in the business model and development plan. He knew the market and had gained the trust of the people in the industry. When that happens, progress is easier.

So, when you have worked in a particular field, you are halfway there because you know the market and the competition. You know the client and the minor details of their work, and the customer knows that you understand their needs.

Continuing on this subject, C.M., the founder and CEO of Veltio, told me a story. Veltio provides software services to retailers and has customers with global well-known market names, such as Tesco and Sainsbury's in the UK, Disney and Forever 21 in the US, and many more.

"I had a good reputation at a company I worked for before I started at Veltio because I was involved at all levels of the product. From technical support, sales to installation, I had acquired a brand. This helped me a lot while setting up my own company—an alternative version of the platform I was working on— because many of the executives in the market I was targeting already knew me. Our first big job was with

Sainsbury's, a very well-known English brand, and it allowed us to enter the competition because they had known me for several years. Our competitors were giants in the field, such as IBM, Accenture, and other big names, which are known worldwide. In other words, 10 to 100 times bigger than us. The proposals in such competitions are up to 250 pages long, covering every area and possible problem they may face in a written plan. We had never done anything like that before. In fact, I had seen very few proposals.

"We decided to do what suited us. We prepared an offer that was 40 pages long. We got the job eventually because we knew the system extremely well. We had set up the original version at our previous workplace.

"Later, the overseers at Sainsbury's told us we'd been given the job because our proposal was 40 pages long and very specific, which proved we knew what we were talking about. At the same time, other companies were submitting long proposals that the technical staff could make neither head nor tail of. They believed we could communicate with each other. The difficulty is always in getting the customer to trust you. The person you are dealing with has to be persuaded to know your product and provide solutions for every situation."

Price is what you pay. Value is what you get.

Warren Buffet,
Investor

Find the Right Price

In August 1811, an international team of European archaeologists led by Charles Cockerell arrived at Figalia in the Peloponnese to plunder the famous Temple of Epicurius Apollo.

A year earlier, sculptures had been seized from the Temple of Aphaia in Aegina when the same team set to work in the Peloponnese.

The archaeologists applied the strategy already tested in Aegina. They arrived with the simple intention of recording and studying the temple. They had not, however, received official permission from the Turks, and their presence provoked a reaction from the local Turkish religious authorities and the inhabitants of the area.

The archaeologists left but remained determined. They knew that the solution to the problem was bribery. Veli Pasha, the son of Ali Pasha of Ioannina, was the Ottoman Governor of the Peloponnese at the time. The Europeans went to see him and asked for the necessary permission for excavation. Veli Pasha gave them the permission but demanded half the haul in exchange. The agreement was made, and the smugglers were provided with laborers, food, and tools.

Within a few weeks, the laborers, guided by the Europeans, discovered 23 marble plaques from the sculptural decoration of the temple depicting scenes from the Battle of the Centaurs and Amazon warriors.

When they had gathered all the finds, the smugglers returned to Veli Pasha, abiding by their agreement. Ali Pasha's son was dissatisfied when he saw the sculptures, expecting gold and precious metals instead.

He considered the archaeological treasure to be of no value. The metopes that had come to light were just bits of marble as far as he was concerned. Veli Pasha was disappointed and refused to take his share of the ruins. Instead, he asked for £400, much less than the actual value of the sculptures.

So, the smugglers took all the treasure having paid a minimal price. They sold the marble plaques at an auction held in Zakynthos, just as they'd done with the sculptures from the Temple of Aphaia in Aegina.

The bidder was the British Museum, which bought the sculptures for £19,000. The historical monument was the first in Greece to be declared a World Heritage Site by UNESCO in 1986.

So, to put a price on a product, you have to know what it's worth to the customer first.

What if it's an innovative product and there's nothing similar on the market? In that case, it can be quite difficult to determine the value.

So how do you decide what to do?

Some say it's not up to you—the price is decided by the market, the competition, the circumstances, and the customer's profit.

Simply consider that at the end of the day, the customer always wants the best quality for the best price. If you can't convince them of that, or that you're offering better value for money than your competitor, you'll lose them. If there is no current competitor, you have to put your product alongside the one that currently meets the same need.

Seth Godin says, "If someone is going to donate $1,000, they should believe it's going to be worth more than $1,000, either in name or prestige, etc. If someone buys your product that costs €1,000, they should definitely believe it's worth more than €1,000. If you don't convince them it's worth more than they're going to spend, or it will be of greater value than the money if they hadn't spent it, don't expect to close the deal."

When value exceeds price, people give money.

Grant Cardone

The famous TV chef, Jamie Oliver's restaurant chain appointed bankruptcy trustees, putting at least 1,300 jobs at risk. He wrote on Twitter:

> "I am deeply saddened by this result and would like to thank all the staff and suppliers who have put their hearts and souls into this business for over a decade."

While the great chef's books and TV shows earned him millions, his restaurants did not live up to expectations. Restaurant critics and industry experts claim that the expensive, poor quality food offered at his three High Street restaurants was a recipe for disaster.

Experts claim that Jamie used his name and reputation to justify the high prices, but it hardly justified the poor quality of the food. In fact, food critic Marina O'Loughlin said that they would have to pay her to eat at his restaurant again.

Market analyst Fiona Cincotta commented that the restaurant chain was powered by the famous name of Jamie Oliver and had been struggling for years to maintain the business model. Pasta, the main Italian dish offered in his restaurants, was too expensive for the middle class and not expensive enough to appeal to celebrities.

The definition of the price of the product, in this case, was wrong. In other words, the wrong pricing often costs the company its existence.

> **΄΄** The moment you make a mistake in pricing, you're eating into your reputation or your profits.

Katharine Paine,
News Group

In his book, *Secrets of Closing the Sale*, Zig Ziglar tells the story of a very capable car salesman.

> *In November 1975, I decided to buy a new car, the new Cadillac 76, which had just been released. I had a great car, but I bought a new car every five to six years.*
>
> *While speaking to a colleague, the conversation turned to cars, and he unreservedly suggested I go to the best salesman he knew—Chuck Bellows. This is what he said:*
>
> *"If Chuck says it's going to rain, get an umbrella. It's going to rain!"*
>
> *"Fine," I replied. "Call him and tell him I'm on my way there now." When I arrived, Chuck was waiting for me at the door. He welcomed me by saying that my car was one of the most beautiful cars ever sold.*

A great way to start a conversation with a potential customer is to compliment them.

> *I thanked him, saying I was really pleased with my car. Chuck continued.*

"Could you tell me where you bought it from?"

I replied that I had got it from a friend who worked for General Motors.

"I can imagine you got a second-hand a company executive had been using, right? And, judging by your ability and your skills, I'm sure you did a very good deal to get it."

"Exactly. The car had just 2,100 miles on the clock, and I bought it for $5,600. I'm very proud of the deal we made as well as the value for money."

"Well," said Chuck, "if it's as good on the inside as it is on the outside, I'm sure we can offer you an excellent part-exchange deal. In fact, I'll call the appraiser right now."

While waiting for the appraiser to do his job, we sat in at the salesman's office and talked. At some point, Chuck asked why I was replacing a great car now, and I replied that in three weeks, I was getting together with my old classmates.

"I'd like to turn up in a new car," I said.

The price was set, and it was high. More than what the buyer wanted to spend. Zig had inadvertently told the salesman how much he'd paid for the car six years ago and how long he had to get a new one.

If I waited for perfection, I would never write a word.

Margaret Atwood,
Poet and Writer

Sell the Idea

I honestly believe that selling is an art. So, the definition of value often requires artistic skills.

Don't hesitate to start talking about your product. Talk from the demo. Even before that, get feedback from friends and acquaintances, interview potential clients, make them believe in your product while you're creating it, and you'll have built a network of loyal followers.

In a conversation I had with G.G., vice president of development at Workable, he said, "The chief mistake with start-ups is that they focus all their attention on creating and developing the product and not on sales. I remember as a cofounder of Incrediblue (an online platform for simplifying the boat rental process) that we lost out on a whole summer because we hadn't finalized the payment issue.

"We could have launched the platform without the payment element the first summer. Just to test it. The feedback alone would have been very important and would have helped us a lot. So, it was a waste of valuable time."

It's usually not a problem of a wrong sale or a hasty move. It's how fast you'll be able to get onto the market and test your product to see if it really sells. It's very nice and creative to develop a good product but as N.M of Workable says, "Start-up founders are great at development. It's the sales that they struggle with."

 The secret of getting ahead is getting started.

Mark Twain,
Author

In the book *This is Marketing,* contemporary marketing guru Seth Godin mentions the following:

It doesn't make any sense to make a key and then run around looking for a lock to open. The only productive solution is to find a lock and then fashion a key. It's easier to make products and services for the customers you seek to serve than it is to find customers for your products and services.

He further added:

Adequate is an excellent place to get started. You go to your potential client for the first time with this to get feedback. This is where you make them think. After noting their remarks and making the necessary corrections and adjustments, you proceed to the next meeting. If you manage to co-create it along with the customer, then you already have a buyer and several recommendations for others.

Recommendations are the best way to approach potential customers. These are the people you will co-create your product with. You request a little of their time, ask what they would like a similar product to have, and ask for their opinion because they are knowledgeable and experienced.

You approach them by saying that you talked with so-and-so (now easy to find on social media), who suggested you should talk to them.

When you meet a potential customer, you explain that the product is not quite ready and not for sale—so there is no reason for them to take a defensive stance—but you want to discuss it with an expert to understand exactly what is needed.

They feel they are helping and, at the same time, are honored by the recognition of their work and knowledge.

Once you have established a relationship of trust, you ask them to recommend someone else in the industry your product is aimed at. This is how one builds the base for a future customer.

Next, it's a good idea to keep them regularly informed about the progress of your product, so when you come to sell it, you've already gained the trust of your future customers.

 You begin by always expecting good things to happen.

Tom Hopkins,
Writer and Speaker

The first thing you do when designing a product is understand why someone would buy it. In his book *Trade Off*, Kevin Maney identifies two main reasons that someone buys a product: Convenience and high fidelity.

Convenience means comfort, fast, reliable, and flexible. People pay more for convenience. High fidelity means high aesthetics, emotional impact, and social status.

However, it is possible to design a product with both these characteristics that eventually fails. A classic example is the Segway, the personal vehicle with two big wheels usually driven by security company employees in large shopping centers.

The company that designed it spent 100 million dollars on research and development. The people who designed it were certain it would revolutionize transportation, in the same way that cars changed the industry after the horse and cart.

When the product finally hit the market, about 10% of the expected customers bought the product. It was a well-designed and functional product, which the market simply rejected.

The message for the product designers was clear.

It's better to create an early version of your product and put it on the market to get feedback than to hide away for a year secretly designing it.

The goal is always the same: gather enough information before creating something the customer will be willing to pay for.

On this very topic, I spoke to Maggie K., cofounder and Lead UI/UX Designer of SimpleApps. The company is active in the field of mobile application development, with clients such as telecommunications companies, TV channels, and other multinational companies and creates its own applications at the same time. We talked about the MVP (Minimum Viable Product), and how ready it needs to be to launch and be tested on the market. Maggie had a very interesting story to tell.

> "In 2013, our first attempt as a start-up was with the development of tourismart, an application for hotels. Hotel guests could gain access to all available hotel services, such as room service, room reservation, activities, etc.
>
> "We became relatively well-known through competitions and awards and bigger clients began to approach us. We are a B2B company. But it wasn't until we developed our first B2C product that we realized our approach to B2B products was wrong. This came about when we developed an application for Pokemon GO.

"But let's go back to the beginning. We started by showing tourismart to potential customers, which at the time were boutique hotels, all-inclusive, large units with swimming pools, activities, etc. "After preparing the product according to *our* specifications, we started on the presentations. It turned out to be a slap in the face for us.

"We had designed a product that met the needs *we* considered hotels had. We hadn't shown it to anyone until then. This was clearly wrong!

"We were creating a product with perfect appearance and functionality and a large variety of features *we* thought would fully cover our potential customers.

"We'd decided to perfect it first and then present it. Clearly a false strategy!

"I remember we had a meeting with a client who owned a boutique hotel in Santorini. It was the ideal refuge for very wealthy customers. The hotelier took a look at it.

"'Well done guys,' he said, 'very nice, very easy to use but something is missing. I'd like my poolside guests to be able to access all services without seeing the staff. The type of guests who come to my hotel may want a towel but without having to ask a nearby member of staff.'

"This was one of the hotel's special features.

"Conclusion? Our design didn't cover the client's basic need, and he would only pay for an application if it provided a solution to *his* problem, not for something *we* thought needed a solution.

"Another problem we encountered was that with our design, the customer's connection to the hotel was their room. The application gave the guests access to information such as how much they had paid for the room, what they had consumed from the mini bar, how much they owed the hotel restaurant, and much more.

"What we had not taken into consideration, however, was that room rates change several times during the day—even within the hour—so the reception had to include these details at check-in, too. This process took about four to five minutes per room. So, for groups of 40 to 50 people, it was virtually impossible.

"We, therefore, had to change the design element that connected the guest to the hotel since the process we had chosen didn't match how the hotel operated.

"Clearly, we should have approached clients earlier to get the appropriate feedback. Maybe we shouldn't have invested in competitions that offered us visibility and credibility on the one hand, but little value regarding the feedback required to create a product someone would pay for on the other.

"We lost valuable time, which could have created other losses. Nowadays, fortunately, the product can be found in more than six hundred hotels across 30 countries around the world.

"This became even more apparent when Pokemon GO came out! At the time, we decided to create an auxiliary-accompanying application for those who played the game. You captured Pokemon characters and with Pokevolution, you tried to develop them to become a better trainer. We were aiming to bring the people playing the game to our application, to benefit from the frenzy of people playing Pokemon GO in the early days. The decision was made immediately—though I had my suspicions—and in six hours, we created the MVP. No one put any more work into it!

"We also decided that if we could offer 10 features, and could prepare just three in one weekend, we would do that and nothing more.

"The MVP worked! It had over 1.5 million downloads in a month. Whenever I went to the office, I must admit I was bullied by my coworkers. The six-hour application and the right timing left us with a very sound profit. Better than that of tourismart.

"This was the answer to the original tourismart design. Don't waste time developing something *you* think is perfect. Get out there with the MVP, get feedback from the market and carry on.

"Now, I would like to give new developers one piece of advice.

"Have someone with business insight on your team. If it's left to us—the developers—we'll create a great product that no one will buy. Developing a product requires a market perspective, too.

"Because no matter how good it is, if you don't sell it, it'll be nothing more than a memory."

Sell yourself first, if you want to sell anything.

Burt Lancaster,
Actor

Sell Yourself and Your Team

In 2019, the Entranet team presented the housemate smart home package, the easiest smart home system in the world.

A high quality, low cost, plug-and-play, voice-controlled smart home system, user-friendly to all, whether they are looking at it or walking about, tech-savvy or not. But it took some convincing to make people believe that this amazing system was not developed by a large company in the industry but by five people from Greece. Even if we weren't directly asked, we still had this question to answer:

How did you do it?

I continued my presentation.

"Three factors:

First, we have an outstanding group of people with both technical and business backgrounds who've been working together for years. A multi-award-winning team.

"It was proclaimed a National Innovation Champion by the European Business Awards, has received the Seal of Excellence from the European Commission, and achieved the highest score in the EU programme for 'Wider: the smart home for the elderly.'

"Second, a few years ago, Entranet designed and developed a worldwide innovation in the smart building area, with talk2lift, the world's first elevator voice control system.

"And third, large companies have already put their trust in us, submitting two subsidized European programs for the development of new products alongside us. The programs have been approved and for the next three years, our company will work closely with well-known brands."

I was, thus, introducing a group of people with recognized value who had gained the trust of successful companies and selected market executives. A company that is, nevertheless, a start-up! With all the pros and cons, of course, that the term implies.

Today, large companies all over the world are buying out start-ups to gain not only a technological edge, but the fresh outlook of people working beyond commitments and rigid structures. Buying out a start-up, of course, is rather expensive and dangerous.

In the end, I said, "In our case, you have all the advantages and none of the risks. We can begin cooperating with mutual and pre-agreed benefits."

According to Forbes magazine, the need to build and sell your team is even greater in the eyes of investors.

Young entrepreneurs often focus on the idea and the business opportunity. They describe how their product is better and smarter.

Realistically speaking, however, the start-up founder is judged by their character, honesty, perceptiveness, and most importantly, their team, as well as their ability to attract 'top players' in their endeavor.

I have often heard that investors will rely more on an excellent group with mediocre ideas than on an excellent idea that a mediocre group will be called upon to implement.

So, in the initial discussions, emphasis will be placed on who will execute the idea, their skills, their background and why the team will deliver on its promises.

T.K., the marketing and communications manager at TEDx, Thessaloniki, insists that marketing is essential, especially if you don't have qualifications.

"The start-up founder should also carry out personal marketing. To develop their image, know where to place themselves in the marketplace. To be able to tell someone who they are and what they're doing in two minutes. Do you know how many start-up founders come here to advertise their work and take 10 minutes to explain what they're doing?"

You don't build a business. You build people and then people build the business.

Melissa Dowie,
Analyst

Haiti, 2005. A country of 11 million people that occupies half of the Spanish island of Hispaniola very close to the USA between Cuba and Puerto Rico.

Haiti is the poorest country in the western hemisphere. Hunger, disease, and misery fill the everyday lives of its inhabitants.

One particular industry, however, is doing well. Kidnapping.

The rationale is simple. If you own a car, you have money to pay a ransom. And if you don't, there's still the car.

A 12-year-old boy was in his father's car when he was abducted. The father had Haitian citizenship, but his son was born in the US and had American citizenship.

The father thought that as soon as he informed the FBI abductions section that an American citizen was in the hands of the abductors, the whole operation would be mobilized immediately and effectively.

He called Washington and the call went through to the person in charge of international abductions, Mr Chris Voss.

The father of the child was disappointed. He thought they'd spring into action at the site of the abduction.

"So, how do you intend to help my son from Washington? Over the phone?" he asked.

Chris Voss knew he had about 10 seconds before the abducted child's father hung up on him. This is what he said:

"Yes. Because for some magical reason, Haitians will kill each other over nothing but they don't kill their kidnap victims. Also, today is Thursday. I know for certain that kidnappers in this area love their Saturday night parties and won't miss them for all the money in the world. If you say what I tell you at the right time, by Friday night, or Saturday morning at the latest, your son will be home."

"Tell me what to do," said the father.

Chris Voss could have mentioned his excellent CV to command respect, but the line would have gone dead in no time.

To communicate with someone, you need to establish a relationship of trust. This, however, takes time. So, if you don't have time, you must show that you know what you're talking about.

And the man on the other end of the line realized that Chris Voss knew what he was talking about.

For the record, the child returned home on Friday night.

You, however, are 25 years old, starting out with no previous experience and need to convince a company executive about yourself and your capabilities. Remember that if you haven't been sleeping 24 hours a day, whatever you did over the past 10 years is probably worth mentioning.

In my first book, *Start-ups: From the Idea to the Global Market,* I spoke to M.M., founder and owner of Brain Up, a business consulting and executive training company, who told me that when he went to university to study Business Administration, he had enough free time to get a job. Or to be precise, various jobs.

One of them was at a summer camp organized by the Ministry of Health.

"In my last year at university, I was Leader in charge. After graduating from university and completing my military service, I was hired by Tasty Foods. My interview had nothing to do with my studies. I told them I knew about statistics, accounting and management and they asked me to tell them about the summer camps. That was how I got my first job."

So, whatever previous experience you have, it's always worth mentioning it, whether you joined a group, managed clients, spoke into a microphone or excelled in a written assignment.

No one expects you to have 23 years of experience when you're 25 years old. And if they do, open the door and leave. Such a meeting would not end well, so don't waste your time. It's relatively simple, of course, to show you are not alone, and that you have a team to back you up in every situation, good or bad.

This team should always be available.

When you call them, they should all be waiting to answer your question, give the right information, and correct any mistakes.

The team must be united.

You could need all kinds of information during the

presentation. If the team behind you responds immediately, the customer is more likely to establish that relationship of trust of their own accord.

 If you are the CEO, you are the brand.

George Farris,
Founder of Liberty National Life Insurance Company

Dataways SA was founded in 2000 by executives with significant experience in the field of telecommunications and information technology. It is now a leading service company with extensive knowledge of infrastructure technologies and famous for the trust shown by its customers in Greece and abroad.

This was not always the case, of course.

The CEO of Dataways told me this.

"In the beginning, I knocked on a lot of doors and took a lot of beatings. Refusals came time after time.

"It's difficult to gain the trust of the person across the table. You have to understand the problems he's facing and not just the superficial ones. You also need to be a bit of a psychologist.

"All you can do is sell yourself. You gain credibility as you go along and from common acquaintances in the marketplace who are willing to give you good references.

"Above all, you need to convince people you can provide a credible solution to their problems.

"In my case, good references from previous employers and associates counted a lot. The marketplace knew I was ethical, had the know-how, and was willing to work.

"I became the guru of the Internet out of nowhere. All the technicians from the companies we'd collaborated with or had just given a presentation to, recommended me for any problem in our field that needed a solution.

"That's how my first job came about.

"Our first project, however, came from a company I used to work for. I had a good reputation with them and recommended Dataways for the best and most cost-effective solution to a problem they were paying rather a lot to solve at the time.

"I sold myself while I was working for this multinational. Without intending to, or even knowing at the time that I'd be setting up a company of my own and getting work from them.

"My old colleagues seemed very pleased that I'd be taking a problem off their hands. As a bonus, they handed us a major client.

"I left with a project that paid off all our expenses and gave us great references for other potential clients. It was a breaking point."

If I'm selling you something, I speak your language. If I'm buying, dann müssen Sie Deutsch sprechen!

Willy Brandt,
Former Chancellor of Germany

Adapt to the Culture

In February 2017, I was in Austin, Texas. I was ready to present Entranet to investors and mentors in the offices of Angelos Angelou's International Accelerator.

After the presentation, we went to Mr Angelo's home, where Greek hospitality remained unchanged, despite his emigration many years before.

At dinner, Angelos told me that he and his wife had decided to stop nine of an unknown number of subscriptions they were paying each month. He said that they hadn't even used those services for at least three years.

So, if this applies to you, you need to make your product compatible with such conditions. On the other hand, a large percentage of European citizens will not subscribe or supply their credit card details even if you give them 30 days for free because they're afraid they'll forget to cancel the subscription, which will incur charges.

Every culture has its own habits, and the start-up founder should adapt accordingly.

If, for example, your job involves getting information from questionnaires, there are things to which people in certain countries will not respond. In America, they will not provide information on alcohol consumption, and the Germans and Belgians do not share information about members of their families.

If a bank manager moves from Berlin to Barcelona and uses the same management methods, their team will not produce the same results.

It's the same when you want to promote a product to different populations. For example, advertising an air conditioning unit in America would emphasize the individual benefits and how the buyer will feel if they buy it. The same unit in South Korea should prove to be greener than the competition's and, therefore, a good choice for the well-being of the society, the country, and the planet.

The book *YES! Fifty Secrets from the Science of Persuasion* tells of a chewing gum advertisement in two different cultures. The individual-orientated advert said, 'Offer yourself the experience of fresh breath!' while the collective-orientated advert said, 'Share the experience of fresh breath!'

A typical case is that of an adventurous businessman who saw a gap in the market on a trip to Africa and decided to open cinemas in various countries of the continent. He even decided to show the most recent Hollywood movies to attract audiences.

After a great advertising campaign, the cinemas remained empty. Over time, he was informed that in these countries, it was unacceptable for men and women to watch a movie or do any other activity together in the same place. Once a dividing line was placed between the male and female seats in the cinemas, they filled up. It's very important to have extensive knowledge of the culture of the country you're trying to export to. It can prove fatal.

On June 5, 1967, the six-day-war began between Israel and its neighboring Arab countries. The hostilities ended five days later, on June 10, with the Israelis triumphant. They won because they had tripled their territory, conquering Sinai, the Gaza Strip, the West Bank, East Jerusalem, and the Golan Heights.

Why am I mentioning this in a book about entrepreneurship? Because years of promoting Ariel detergent in the Arab world went to waste.

The hero of the war was the leader of the Israelis, Ariel Sharon. Consequently, Palestinians, Egyptians, Syrians, and Jordanians would not buy a product that bore his name.

So, if you decide to export to foreign markets, you need to be careful. Even with the name you decide to give your product. Don't cause offense where customs and traditions are concerned. Don't choose an objectionable or offensive name.

Baron Marcel Bich, founder and owner of BIC, followed this rule.

The story begins when Hungarian journalist, Laszlo Biro, made a new tip for his fountain pen consisting of a freely rotating ball in a tube after seven years of trial and error. When the ball was put to paper, it evenly spread ink from an inner tube. Laszlo had created the biro!

The first generation of the pen was not perfect. The metal ball often leaked, and the ink stalled. Most of Laszlo's customers returned the pens leading the company to near bankruptcy. Laszlo sold his biro rights in Europe and the United States for the company to survive.

The European who bought the rights to the pen was Frenchman, Marcel Bich.

Marcel adored pens and when, in 1950, he heard that Laszlo was selling the patent, he paid two million dollars for it. He modernized the production and bought raw materials in bulk, which allowed him to sell the product at a very low price.

Initially, Bich wanted to name the pen after his surname, but when he was told how English-speaking countries pronounced it, he decided to remove the h.

Thus, Bic was born, and it still sells more than seven billion pens a year.

O.M., founder of ORAMA Group, an Athens-based communications company, agreed with the role local customs play.

Early in his career, he had several jobs, most of them in the sales sector. He shared, "In 2012, I was in the sales department of a software company. Some Russian customers came to the office, we presented the product and decided to continue the conversation over dinner. We went to a restaurant, and they ordered vodka with the food.

"I was aware of the culture because I had just returned from a trip to the northeast of Europe, doing market research and analysis. Also, due to my age, I went to several parties and events, some of which were in a student environment. I knew these people's customs, and my stomach had grown used to it.

"That night, however, I reached my limit. I couldn't refuse to carry on because I'd done it once before and noticed how their mood changed. It was as if I'd offended them. And I was there on behalf of my firm. I had to respect their culture, which says that if you don't drink the first glass of vodka, you offend them and if you don't drink the ones that follow, you're not man enough to do business with them. If you don't drink the final glass, by which time everyone's either a little or very drunk, they take it personally.

"So, I went along with it as best I could. I don't even remember how the night ended.

"The next day, I couldn't get out of bed. I'd had countless calls from the owner of the company and dragged myself to the office. At a very relaxed pace, to be honest. Not only because I thought the deal was over, but also because I expected to arrive at the office and wait to be called into the accounts department for a thank you note for my services.

"The customers were already at the office. Very fresh—they probably did it this often and certainly more often than me—and very cheerful. They were already talking to the owner of the company, who was very happy because the deal was done.

"The only job I closed at the time, was this one. Because I respected the customer's culture and they appreciated it."

> If you respect the language and the culture, it shows in your work.
>
> **A. R. Rahman,**
> Music Producer

I bring this chapter to an end by going back 77 years. In March 1945, World War II came to an end. Japan is all but destroyed.

After the end of the war, Navy Lieutenant Masaru Ibuka and Weapons Researcher Akio Morita looked everywhere for work. Masaru found work in a department store where he repaired radios. In 1946, he persuaded Akio and several of his friends to start a business together.

They borrowed $530 as start-up capital and founded Tokyo Telecommunications Engineering Corporation or Totsuko for short.

Despite its name, the company did not have the budget for a research department for the development of telecommunications, and so, their first product was a device for cooking rice. It did not sell at all, and very soon, Masaru left the home appliance market.

His first success came in 1949 when he tested a cassette player, imported from the USA by the Japan Broadcasting Corporation. Cassette players were a very new technology at the time and Totsuko became the number one in the Japanese market.

In 1950, a G-type recorder was released. Although the sales were initially low, when the Japanese economy began to recover, Totsuko's fortunes changed. Then, in 1952, Masaru came up with a universal invention that would change the world: the transistor.

It had been invented five years earlier by Bell Laboratories but was used, almost exclusively, by the military. Masaru immediately saw the potential of the transistor and did whatever it took to get his hands on it. He managed to get a technology licence from Western Electric for $25,000, a price so high that it almost bankrupted Totsuko.

Masaru risked everything and in 1955, Totsuko successfully created Japan's first transistor, the TR-55.

It was a remarkable achievement. Not only did they create a radio that was small and portable, but they also managed to improve transistor technology.

They saw a great opportunity to sell their radio, not only in Japan, but also in the USA, where the market was much bigger and equally unexploited.

However, to attract the Americans, Totsuko had to find a trademark. They appropriately got their name from the Latin word sonus, which means sound.

So, in 1955, Sony was born.

It was the first time a Japanese company would use a foreign name with western origins!

Morita, however, believed that if he wanted to expand into the world market, the name should be simple, easy to understand and easy to pronounce in all languages.

Mission accomplished!

An idiot with a plan can defeat a genius without a plan.

Warren Buffett

Make a Marketing Plan

Athens, 2012. Dimitri M. started a business venture creating Poqa Olive Oil, an extra premium olive oil designed to cover a niche market with amazing packaging similar to that of a perfume. It was his first association with the food industry. Dimitri, founder and CEO of Yamas, had been in sales for 20 years.

"The quality of the local olive oil is excellent, but we sell it mainly to Italians who standardize it, package it and market it all over the world. In Greece, standardization is practically non-existent and targeted exports are minimal, so I was very motivated by this. The question is: 'Can we compete with the Italians and Spanish who have dominated the global supermarket sector for years?' Obviously, we can't."

He goes on to explain how and why he decided to deal in something different, a distinctive luxury food targeting a specific market.

"Our plan was clear. We imagined the type of customer that would buy this product and had decided on the stores that could sell it. There was just one problem. They were world-famous stores, the ones the whole world wanted to visit because of their reputation. Stores like Harrods, Selfridges and all the global well-known names.

"I went to Paris to do the initial market research and make some connections. I was almost totally unprepared, had no scheduled meetings to go to, and no knowledge of the operating framework. In short, I had no idea of the process of how to schedule a meeting as a potential supplier, who in the hierarchy to contact, how long the process would take, who sets the prices, etc. I had no idea at all!

"But I did have a plan, which said that to sell to that particular food sector, I would have to put the product on the shelves of Harrods and Galeries Lafayette.

"So, I visited Galeries Lafayette in Paris with no appointment, no business cards, no brochures, not even the product.

"'Good morning,' I said, '*Bonjour*,' they replied. I asked to speak to the manager of the store and some of them looked at me nervously, trying to understand what the serious problem was and why a customer was asking to see the manager.

"A girl told me the store manager was absent, but she might be able to help me. I asked if we could go to an office to talk, and the awkwardness continued. This was not normal behavior for either a customer or indeed a supplier.

"I wanted to create the right environment to tell my story. I wasn't properly prepared, but this is a basic principle of sales.

"In the office, I told her I marketed olive oil and wanted to work with them. She laughed, of course, and said that was not how the system worked. 'Do you have it with you?' she asked. I said I did not, and she laughed again. 'Can I see it somewhere? Do you at least have a website?'

"We did have a website and I made sure it was in French as well. She really liked it because the packaging was impressive, and she thought they could stock it. I come from a village where it's customary to ask about the origins of anyone we meet. I always ask where someone comes from. It may seem a bit strange to ask a Galeries Lafayette executive where she comes from, but I did anyway.

"It turned out that Alexandra was a Serb. I hugged her, said our people are like brothers and that we should be comfortable in each other's company. I told her my story and that my company was a start-up and she wanted to help us as much as she could.

"Indeed, two months later, we had our first meeting with the stock manager. We managed to avoid all the usual procedures, such as waiting for six to eight months to be seen, the competition, etc. and gave a presentation that went extremely well. In the end, we were given the green light by Galeries Lafayette.

"It was the beginning of an amazing journey. It was much easier to be accepted by other global luxury stores after that. And so we were. By Harrods, Selfridges, and Bon Marché.

"Looking back, I realize I was oblivious to the risk. I was aiming high but in uncharted waters.

"On the other hand, that was my strategy. Aim high and create a brand for my product.

"While I was designing it with the graphic designer, he asked me where I was going to sell it.

"I told him I wanted a product fit for Galeries Lafayette and Harrods, and we'd see about the rest later because if I could sell it there, I could sell it anywhere.

"I had no idea if it was right or wrong at the time, but the strategy was pretty clear. I knew what I had to do; I just had to find out how to do it. Today, I can say that the plan was absolutely successful."

Every minute you spend in planning saves ten minutes on execution; this gives you a 1000% return on energy.

Brian Tracy,
Writer and Executive Trainer

To create a marketing plan, you need to know what marketing is. So, I asked T.K., CEO of Metagenesis Advertising.

"Marketing is four things:

First. Which product, which service will I offer, the market research involved, and how I will put it on the market.

"Second and very important, how much will I sell it for? What's the right price for this product on the market?

"Third, its position in the marketplace. Do you know how many companies advertise and have no availability in the marketplace? They launch campaigns, spend money, the consumer goes in search of the product and when they can't find it, the product is dead.

"Fourth, promotion. Promotion, advertising, and people. People are very important today. People who work for the products, those who work in businesses, those who work in advertising."

Amid all the chaos, how do you get the message across? Just as I thought: Consistency and continuity.

"On average, each of us receives more than 5,000 messages from the time we wake up to the time we go to sleep.

"I wake up . . . I get up . . . I see something . . . I switch on my mobile, I receive a message. I get dressed, listen to music, or listen to the news, and get another message—my wife is telling me something. I go out on the street, I see a billboard, I turn on the radio, I listen to more messages, an interview, advertisements. These are all messages.

"Amid this throng of messages, you need to be able to do two things: stand out and innovate. Be able to say something different.

"Beyond that, and according to how much money you have, the intensity of the message comes into play.

"OK, if you have \$1,000, you'll spend \$1,000. Spend it right. And spend it again a month later, three months later, six months later. And when you spend it again, say the same thing. The amount you have decided on is relative to where you want to place your product.

"Who am I, what do I want, what is my competitive advantage, who are my customers?

"Do I know who my customers are? What will I tell them? How do I tell them? How intense is my message? What resources do I have? How much money can I spend?

"What do I want the consumer to think about me when he hears the name of my product or business?

"This is very important because you can say the same thing 50 times in different ways (with a photo, a video, another video, a spot in a magazine, a message on the radio). In the end, however, all these messages must have the same target. To get the same message across to the consumer.

"This, in turn, will add value to the money invested.

"If one day you say you're handsome, the next you say you're tall, the next you say you're smart, the message is lost. And you've lost your reliability too. Because you are confusing!

"Let's say you have 100 punch lines. How will you deliver them, what will you say?

"You must get the same message across with all 100 of them. If the first 20 deliver one message and the next 20 another, you have 20 punch lines, not 100. It's, therefore, very important to be consistent and continuous in your messaging. It will also give you cumulative value."

Yiannis K., Commercial director of expert international, seems to share this view:

"A company, but more specifically its marketing plan, needs consistency. In everything it says. When a product is advertised, used by the customer or, in our case, when someone comes into the store, the message must be the same.

"There is always a gap between customer expectation via a communication route and the actual in-store experience or when using a product. Expectation is usually somewhat better than the actual experience.

"If the gap is small, the customer justifies it and overcomes it. If it is large, they fall into it. A company marketing plan should have the elements that I try to pass on to my daughter:

"P.C.P.—Persistence, Focus, Patience.

"You have set a goal. Of course, you listen and take other information on board and make the necessary adjustments. But if you have a goal and a plan, don't be influenced by the voices telling you to change them."

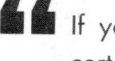 If you don't succeed with your marketing plan, you certainly wouldn't have succeeded without one.

Anonymous

On the other hand, of course, you can have the best plan that doesn't work out. Or not have a plan and favorable conditions prove your product a success. But this is the exception to the rule.

A few years ago, a motorcycle spare parts business in Thessaloniki decided to import scooters. The owner asked his advertising company to prepare a big campaign. Radio, social networks, and television.

The work began. A few weeks later, the design and costing were ready. But in the meantime, dockworkers had gone on strike. The business owner received his order 45 days later than expected.

The scooter is a seasonal product. As soon as it starts to rain, sales drop. The team decided not to run the campaign and even though the scooters arrived out of season, they sold like hotcakes.

As far as cost-effectiveness was concerned, the market responded with enthusiasm. No one could have predicted it.

The point is, that if the campaign had run, the business owner would have thought the advertising company did all the work or the slogan was a complete success. As it turned out, this was not the case, but it might just have been a coincidence.

On the other hand, some huge companies spend large amounts on marketing campaigns without the desired effect.

In my first book, I talked about McDonald's and the New Coke. Groups had tested the products and behavioral analysis had been done by experts, but no one expected them to fail. Samsung is a more recent case.

Samsung believed the market would back curved TVs. It invested heavily in research and development, production, and advertising, but also a commercial orientation in this direction.

Samsung thought that since these screens were very successful with gamers, they would also be popular with a large percentage of the market.

However, the video game player profile is different to that of the general public. If gamers were given the choice, they'd choose 360° screens for full, live participation in the game. This is not the case with everyone though, as they soon found out.

Three years later, Samsung started producing one curved TV model, though according to their plan, it would have accounted for 60% of their production.

> " Fifty percent of promotion ends up in the rubbish bin. I just don't know which 50%.

Old saying

Today more than ever, adaptation and flexibility are required. Any change in social network algorithms requires direct action by marketing and communication teams. We're living in the age of social media influencers, YouTubers, and vloggers, who have invested in achieving exactly this, and are capable of launching your product or service.

Game of Thrones is the most successful series in the history of television. At the 68th Emmy Awards, it won 37 awards.

That's the highest number of Emmy Awards for a fiction series ever. In total, the series has won 47 Emmys out of a total of 128 nominations.

According to Parrot Analytics, the series was 159 times more popular than the average television program.

The final episode of the fifth season also set a record for the most viewers sharing a particular file at the same time: 258,131 downloads. And for about eight million viewers in the US, this was the most successful season.

The crew of the series, of course, left nothing to chance. They considered several factors in their choice of actors. Two girls were selected for a crucial role. One was the better actress, the other had a million followers on social media. Who do you think got the role?

At the same time, advertising can be completely personalized these days. You can approach 25 to 50-year-old Estonian civil engineers with a specific message for a minimal amount and go public any time you choose. But despite the tools available to contemporary marketers, a recent survey showed that 85% of marketing campaigns fail to get the message across.

One thing stays the same: everyone is competing for the consumer's attention and advertising costs everyone the same. So, what do you do?

Seth Godin, in his book *The Purple Cow*, uses a successful metaphor to demonstrate this principle of modern marketing:

Suppose you're driving along the highway and you see a field full of brown cows. Ordinary and boring. If you suddenly saw a purple cow among them, your eyes would focus on it straightaway. It would conjure up various expectations and attract your attention. If you attract a person's attention, you can move on to the next stage, the sale!

So, we must ask ourselves:
- How do we attract the customer's attention?
- How do we stand out from the crowd?

A sales team armed with content is a sales team that can more effectively close deals.

Hana Abaza,
Marketing Director of Shopify Plus

Stand Out
from the Crowd

You check your emails in the morning. You find 30 messages from unknown people and start deleting them. Some of them are serious. If they don't stand out, you throw them in the bin and never think about them again. So, how do you stand out from the crowd? How do you get your message across without ending up in the bin?

Look at yourself. Which emails do you open? The ones that interest you. The brief ones. Those that don't require too much of your time. Maybe even those with a short title addressed to you and the body of the email says something like:

'I do this, I want that, I'm asking for x minutes of your time. Let me know when you're available.'

If you expand too much, the email is deleted. The same happens if the potential client doesn't immediately understand the subject and reason for communication.

By simply observing yourself, you can see how to stand out from the crowd.

Randy Garner, a social scientist, did a very interesting experiment. He asked a mixed selection of people to answer a questionnaire. He stuck a yellow Post-it with a personal message on one group of questionnaires, in another, a handwritten message on the questionnaire itself, and in a third, there was just the questionnaire.

The result? Seventy-five percent of the first group responded, 48% of the second, and 36% of the third.

He then decided to prove that the percentage difference between the first two groups was not due to the bright yellow color of the Post-it.

So, he followed up with a second experiment, in which the second group was given questionnaires with a blank Post-it and no notes. The results revealed the intended outcome. Sixty-nine percent of the first group and 43% of the second group completed the questionnaires. Why?

According to Garner, pasting a handwritten note on any letter makes people recognize and appreciate the extra effort the personal gesture adds, and feel the need to reciprocate.

Other variations of the experiment showed that personal notes accompanied by a 'thank you' motivated people, not only to answer the questionnaire but spend more time completing it and return it quicker, providing more information and details. The study's message is clear. The more personalized your communication is, the more likely you are to get a positive response.

This is what Alec Brownstein achieved in 2010, using tons of ingenuity. What did he do? He paid Google to show his ad every time that six selected giant advertising executives typed their names into a search engine. Brownstein claimed he was relying on their vanity and correctly assumed that those particular successful people would often search for what was being said and written about them on the Internet. The ad was there to redirect them to his page.

One of his 'victims' was Ian Reichenthal, who immediately came across Brownstein's promotion when he entered his name in the search bar.

It goes without saying that he offered him an interview and eventually hired him at his advertising company. Brownstein, in his 30s at the time, immediately became the star of the advertising world with this experiment, and he didn't just leave it at that. Today, he is creative director at a global advertising company, and an award-winning writer and director. Is the need to differentiate, however, simply a modern-day phenomenon?

In 1876, Joseph Lister, a distinguished English surgeon, argued in a speech at a medical conference that bacteria floating around operating theaters were the main reason for the high death rate of patients undergoing surgery.

At the time, the mortality rate of those who had surgery was 90%. No one understood that the patients died because of the germs transmitted by the people who were trying to save them. Doctors in those days operated without gloves and operation theaters were open to the public.

After the speech, some of Lister's colleagues mocked him, while others were not convinced by what he had said. Robert Johnson listened carefully though, and was very impressed.

He persuaded his two brothers to leave the pharmaceutical company they had founded a few years earlier and set up a new company to meet the needs created by such new discoveries. Johnson and Johnson was founded and supplied doctors with plasters and gauze that saved thousands of patients from death.

However, to get the message across, he chose a different campaign. He published a manual and a plethora of magazines and books on the new methods of antiseptic wound protection, which were read by doctors to keep up with developments in their field. In times of limited knowledge and information, these publications were the surgeon's bible. Johnson and Johnson's logo and products were always discreetly included at the end.

In the comedy movie Airplane! the pilot becomes seriously ill, and a former army pilot with PTSD undertakes to land the plane. He talks to the control tower, where a veteran army inspector tries to help him.

At some point, the inspector asks,

"Should I turn on the runway lights?"

And the pilot answers,

"No! That's exactly what they're expecting us to do."

A message comes across via the insanity of the film. This is exactly what often happens. To stand out from the crowd, do something that nobody is expecting you to do.

 Chase the vision, not the money. The money will end up following you.

Tony Hsieh,
CEO of Zappos

In his book *Delivering Happiness*, Tony Hsieh says:

> *About a year before we sold Zappos to Amazon, we started a different brand promotion strategy. My colleagues and I began to speak at conferences throughout America. The result of this move was that a much larger and more diverse audience got to know about us than had previously been targeted until then, but also, we shared the stage with prestigious names such as Bill Gates, Larry Page, and many others.*
>
> *At the same time, it gave us the opportunity to personally get to know the conference organizers and that led to even bigger events such as those of SXSW and Tony Robbins.*

Personally, I have been following this example for years. But after my TEDx talk and the publication of my first book, I truly realized the power of a different approach when promoting a company brand and the alternative ways of standing out and conveying your message.

For example, I remember that after many attempts to meet the CEO of a very large company, I gave up. I decided to waste no more time on it and just wait for the right opportunity. It came when we served as panelists at a high-level conference where we were both speakers. It's much easier to be handed a business card and be remembered by someone if they watch you speak or serve on the same panel as you. They'll most likely remember you for a long time afterwards.

One Sunday morning, I met George M., the CEO of Comquent, at a cafe. After telling me about his company, we talked about more personal issues. I discovered that George had a story worth telling.

"I grew up in Germany and in 2006, after completing my studies, I returned to Greece with my wife. I am an electrical engineer; my wife is a civil engineer.

"We decide to move to Thessaloniki, where she comes from. Accustomed to Germany, I imagined I'd find a job relatively quickly and easily. I'd email my CV accompanied by a short text. I knew the situation and wanted my first job after graduating to be linked to the subject I'd studied so as not to lose touch.

"The result was disappointing. I submitted dozens of applications but was rarely invited for an interview. Companies didn't even send negative responses.

However, I didn't give up and called someone in charge at the human resources department to ask if there were any vacancies and if my application had been processed.

"I came to the conclusion that I'd have to change tactics and find a way to stand out from the other candidates, so this is what I did.

"I focused on three companies my research had shown were growing and were relevant to the area I wanted to work in.

"I stayed home for a week and perfected my CV. I wrote letters that were always tailored to the particular company and job I was interested in. I sent them to three friends to review and incorporated their comments.

"I ordered specific A4 CV files from abroad, which were three consecutive pages that folded in from the left and right. So, when someone opened the folder from the left, they had to open the third page as well, but to the right. So, three pages unfolded in front of them. The cover letter was on the left, the CV in the middle and my degree on the right.

"I decided not to post them but deliver them in person. I dressed accordingly and asked for the person in charge of checking CVs and handed over the file with my application in person. None of the companies allowed me to speak directly to the HR manager, so I ended up handing them to the secretary or the accounts department. When I left, I always felt my file would reach the right hands because I had handed it in personally.

"Three days later, my phone rang. At last, I was being called for an interview. After the formal greeting, the first thing the manager said was:

"'I received the file with your CV, and I must confess, I have never seen anything like it before. My first impression, as well as the details in the cover letter, grabbed my attention. And for that reason alone, I had to meet you.'

"The interview went well and two weeks later, I started to work."

He finished by saying, "I think if I'd done the conventional thing, I'd still be looking for a job."

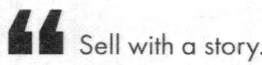 Sell with a story.

Paul Smith,
Fashion Designer

Tell Your Story

Philip, a child from a large family, was born and raised in the suburbs of New York. Today he is 69 years old, retired for the last 18 months, father of three children and grandfather.

Maria is Italian, 42 years old, married, mother of two and works for a large construction company in Birmingham.

Kaito is a 27-year-old programmer living in his hometown of Tokyo.

All of them have one thing in common.

All three are witnesses to the world's greatest population surge since the beginning of humanity.

It all started after World War II, when people felt everything would improve, and their lives would get better.

And it did indeed improve! This optimism led to more children per family. Children born in 1950, like Philip, reached retirement age in 2015.

The problem arises when Philip's children, who are Maria's age, by the way, decided that one or two children are more than enough.

The problem is exacerbated by people of Kaito's generation, who have distanced themselves from the concept of family, preferring 'virtual' to real life.

Let the numbers speak . . .

In 2017, the number of people on earth was seven billion. In 2050, it will be close to $10 billion.

Today, 80% of the developed world lives in cities. In 2050, 80% of the world's population will live in cities. Every day, a city of the size of Oslo will be created.

Cities will double in size, in number or by a combination of the two. By the end of the century, the earth's population will reach 11 billion.

Note: children account for around two billion today and that number will stay the same throughout the whole of the 21st century.

So obviously, we are heading for a society of the elderly. If properly taken advantage of by humanity, it will not be a problem but a challenge to build a better society for all.

Entranet has the solution.

Entranet created a smart home system, easy to use by everyone, for the remote control and operation of functions of the home which can be operated by all users, regardless of their ability to see or get about. Whether they are tech-savvy or not. A smart home environment that improves everyone's life!

Now, let's look at this from a different angle. Entranet created the easiest smart home system in the world. The easiest for the user and the installer. Demographic developments require new products to provide solutions to people's daily lives.

Let the numbers speak.

Which of the two descriptions would you remember the next day? How many people do you think would remember Entranet after the second pitch?

 People do not buy goods and services. They buy relations, stories, and magic.

Seth Godin
Marketing Expert

You've done everything you could. You've put your heart and soul into your idea. You've worked 15 hours a day and weekends. You created your own website, your Facebook page, your YouTube channel, you created content, SEO, and added in the right keywords and . . . nobody cares . . . you have achieved nothing.

So, you think, *'What's going on? What else should I do?'*

Gary Vaynerchuk, author of bestsellers *Crush It and Crushing It*, believes there has never been a better time to start a business.

> *The cost is minimal. The cost of getting your message across to the customer is lower than ever. Facebook Live, YouTube, Snapchat, LinkedIn, Twitter. The problem is that the same is true for everyone. So, everyone does it. As a result, it's more difficult than ever to get someone to care about what you say and interact with you. And nothing conventional will work until one thing is understood.*
> *The story matters!*
> *Maybe you did what you had to do. What the manuals said. Whatever the latest trends demand, all the clever tricks for the algorithm to upload you and the result is zero.*

Gary Vaynerchuk thinks all of the above is just noise with no story behind it. Because you can make a thousand mistakes in the way you communicate, but if you tell your story correctly, people will listen.

The fact is there is no easy or smart way or the right methodology. Nor, as you already realize, a money tree. The only thing that seems to work every time is the story.

Because that's the way to connect with people. Amid the general commotion, you have to connect with the person sitting opposite you for them to hear you.

Think of your customer. Chances are, you're not

putting yourself in their shoes. If you were, you'd see they were living a story recounting their lives.

As the CEO of a start-up, you need to understand them well.

What keeps them awake at night?

What kind of future are they dreaming of?

Your role is to help them get there. And you'll do that by creating a story that'll allow them to change their lives. You're giving them a map that will lead to their goal.

Your customers will buy your product for one reason. They believe it will help them build a better future.

Your job is to cover that need.

 Tell the story of the mountains you climbed. Your words could become a page in someone else's survival guide.

Morgan Harper Nichols
Musician

Storytelling is an ancient process. Our brains are designed to receive information in sequence.

So, when you tell your story, make sure it has a beginning, a middle and an end. And always remember that the listener tends to remember the beginning and the end. So, those messages should be much stronger. If you make a lukewarm start aiming to save the juiciest parts for later, you'll probably lose the customer.

You'll also need to tell your story, so they remember what you said. You have to make them feel, and never forget to add the 'iceberg' to your story.

What would the Titanic be without the iceberg? A cruise. A ship that carried people from Southampton to New York.

Would you have heard of it? Would James Cameron have made a movie about it? Would Leonardo DiCaprio have starred in it, or would it have won 11 Oscars if it was a movie without an emotional climax?

Of course, your story doesn't have to end like the Titanic. But it must contain something to be remembered for. An important event. An extraordinary situation. Something you can build on.

As a start-up founder, you have to convince your customers that you're special enough to be trusted. You have little experience of the marketplace and have neither the big customers nor the big successes to minimise the risk of the person you are asking to trust you.

There are three stories we usually tell.

Start with your personal story: Who you are, where you come from and where you are going. Mention anything related to the target industry of your product, so the other person trusts you. They need to realize you are experienced in the field and are aware of the problems. Often, it helps if you mention people you've worked with.

The story you narrate should be a personal one. Talk about either about yourself or your company. Be careful though. It should not contain personal triumphs. Quite the opposite. It's not a bad idea to relate a personal dilemma. Talk about unfortunate times or even luck but not about ability. Refer to the random event that led you to a conclusion. Your story should include your good points. How you endured the hardships and carried on. Show how you've been through similar situations to those of your client and you feel their pain.

Continue with something to create a connection and trust that shows authenticity. Once you have done this, you can start selling.

Once you start selling, the story changes. It should now contain elements they can also use to sell the idea to their superiors, partners, and/or customers.

The conclusion requires a success story. A story about one of your customers that is not a competitor of theirs. Tell them what they achieved and where are they today because of it. This answers the potential client's question as to why they should do business with you.

 Marketing is no longer about the stuff you make but the stories you tell.

Seth Godin
Marketing Expert

The award-winning *Mad Men* series aired on the American cable channel AMC and won the public's and the critics' approval for its historically authentic representation of the era.

Mad Men takes place in 1960s America at the offices of Sterling Cooper Advertising on Madison Avenue in New York. The title of the series comes from 'Ad Men', which was used by the advertisers of the time for their own purposes. One episode of the series sees the advertisers gather in the meeting room to scrutinize US presidential candidates—Kennedy and Nixon's TV spots.

The first part is simple:

The president is a product. Do not forget this.

Nixon is leading in the polls, but Kennedy is a much more popular 'product' and he is dangerously catching up. The group looks for ways to 'widen the gap' again. A proposal is made to dig up some 'dirt' from Kennedy's past and expose him to the public. On the other hand, the legendary advertiser Don Draper suggests.

"Why damage his reputation when there's a story to tell? Kennedy is a wealthy, well-brought-up, second-generation American. Nixon started from zero. Self-created. He is the Abraham Lincoln of California, who became Vice President of the United States just six years after retiring from the navy. In Kennedy, I see a silver spoon. In Nixon, I see myself!"

The proposal was rejected. Kennedy was filming spots with smiling children and healthy, handsome parents while Nixon was talking about 'dollars and cents'. The election was a walk in the park for John F. Kennedy and his team.

Be clear about your goal but be flexible about the process of achieving it.

Brian Tracy

Creativity and Flexibility

Egypt was one of Alexander the Great's conquests. When he entered the country in 332 BC, its people welcomed him as a liberator and recognized him as the successor of the Pharaohs.

Ptolemy was designated supreme governor of Egypt after the death of Alexander in 323 BC in Babylon and was responsible for the fragmentation of its vast state. In 305 BC, he proclaimed himself King Ptolemy I and later became known as the 'Saviour'.

He proved to be a worthy successor to the throne, protected education and the arts and built the renowned library of Alexandria, which housed a million works in its time of glory, and the museum where philosophers and poets were hosted and collaborated. He died in 283 BC.

Ptolemy II, who went down in history as Philadelphus, because he left his wife to marry his sister Arsinoe, built the Lighthouse of Alexandria while protecting education and the arts equally as effectively as his father.

These two kings laid the foundations for the 'Alexandrian' age to flourish and develop to its fullest.

King Ptolemy II was a spiritual leader and very proud of his library. At the time, another spiritual leader, Eumenes King of Pergamon, also owned a remarkable library.

Papyrus came from the stalk of a plant that grew solely on the banks of the Nile, so Ptolemy banned the export of papyrus to damage the competition, meaning only Egypt could continue to build its library. An embargo was imposed on its competitors.

Papyrus had very specific characteristics. It always had to be rolled, wasn't very durable, was difficult to transport and any extended text needed to fit on the specific papyrus.

Eumenes was forced to look for other solutions. And the market usually provides them. Sheepskin was the alternative. You could write on both sides of the treated leather but also join numerous skins together. The first book in history was, thus, created. Best of all, sheep were everywhere, not just in one country.

So that's how pergamine (parchment) was invented.

Change, before you have to.

Jack Welch
Former CEO of General Motors

Creativity and flexibility have always been the tools of entrepreneurs, either with start-ups or traditional companies.

In 1953, Joseph Stalin died. He is succeeded by Nikita Khrushchev as leader of the powerful Soviet Union. Wanting to show how different he was from his predecessor, he decides to open the border and host an exhibition of American products in Russia.

In the summer of 1959, 450 American companies exhibited their products on Soviet soil. One of them was Pepsi.

US Vice President Robert Nixon also visited the exhibition. On a walk with Khrushchev, they stopped at a booth for a Pepsi. Their photograph made the front pages of American and Russian newspapers the following day.

It took Pepsi 10 years to make its first sale on Soviet territory because there was one serious problem. The Soviet currency was the rouble, which was only valid in the USSR. It had no value in the rest of the world. After negotiations, an agreement was reached. For every bottle of Pepsi sold in the Soviet Union, Pepsi would receive the equivalent amount of Stolichnaya vodka.

The agreement was a huge success. At least for a while. Because there was only so much vodka Americans could consume.

The agreement needed to be amended.

In the spring of 1989, Pepsi's export manager Donald Kendall announced the big news: Pepsi would become the new owner of 17 submarines, a frigate and two more ships.

For a few days, until they were sold for scrap, Pepsi was the seventh-largest naval power in the world.

When Kendall was asked by Congress to explain exactly what kind of agreement had been made with the Soviet regime, he replied, "We are disarming the Soviet Union faster than you."

Pepsi continues to thrive in Russia today, although, after the breakup of the Soviet Union, Coca Cola moved quickly and bought most of the bottling factories for a small percentage of their value.

The well-known Marlboro cigarette brand also had to become particularly flexible. In 1847, Philip Morris opened his first tobacco shop in London. After a few years, he had made a good name for himself in the marketplace and at the end of the century, he was appointed official tobacco supplier to Queen Victoria. In 1902, after the death of the company's founder, the new owners decided to open a tobacco and cigarette store in New York. One of the brands they promoted was Marlboro, 'the female cigarette'.

Yes, exactly! Marlboro started out as a cigarette for women. It had a red filter so lipstick marks were invisible, and its slogan was 'Mild as May'. The ads pictured a woman in a velvet environment.

The market skyrocketed at some point. But for Marlboro, sales were stable in a growing market. Then everything changed!

The war had just ended and there was a large group of 'white collar' workers—veterans who had found work behind a desk. The need arose for them to feel independent again—strong, men, warriors.

The figure of the cowboy, the Marlboro man, was just what they needed. The ad came out in 1955. Sales rose by 3,000%.

Along the way, however, in 1971, a new piece of legislation would test Philip Morris' ability to adapt again. Cigarette advertising was banned, and everyone expected a fall in demand.

Then the Hollywood movies came, where the leading role always smoked Marlboro, and with major sporting events such as the Marlboro sponsored Grand Prix, the Marlboro brand appeared on the screen around 6,000 times, just in one race.

 Be so good they can't ignore you.

Steve Martin
Actor

Of course, there are stories about flexibility all around the world. Such a story was told to me by Jaco Carasso, founder and CEO of Agnotis, an online platform selling diapers and natural care products for babies. We went back a few years to when he and his associates created the auction site, dealingers.

"We went through all the madness start-ups go through. We hit the market in 2011 and after a lot of publicity, we won tenders, got money from investors and a lot of users. No money, just a lot of users.

"At some point, we decided to leave for Silicon Valley. It took us a month to make the decision and we did no market research and had no specific plan. In our minds, dealingers was unique and our native country was a very small market. We were very young and living the dream. In the United States, it was just public relations. Time passed, however, and the money ran out. We returned, realising we had made a mistake. Because of that mistake, however, we came up with the next idea on which Agnotis was based.

"At the time, the 'dollar shave club' was a great success. A guy was selling subscription razors and had a turnover of 200 million in its second year of operation. It was later sold to Unilever for a billion.

"That's where the idea for Agnotis came from and we entered the market for baby products. As we progressed with dealingers, we kept our eyes peeled and our ears to the ground. We were forced to move beyond the scope of the first concept but held on to the digital advertising part, which we knew well by then, but we changed the business idea."

In the end, he said, "If we'd kept the original idea, if we hadn't been flexible enough, we wouldn't be here today."

I like to think of sales as the ability to gracefully persuade, not manipulate, a person or persons into a win-win situation.

Bo Bennett
Author

Michael N. is an entrepreneur and author of the book *Brand. The Strategy.* Michael believes that you cannot create a brand for a product—whatever it is—if you do not associate it with an experience or a feeling.

"Even a drawing pin. The person who buys it is left with the result of the drawing pin and how it will make them feel. A mental image. Maybe they want to hang a picture of their daughter's first birthday on the wall. It's your responsibility to make that connection successfully and efficiently," he said.

He quotes the example of Michelin, and how a tyre company managed to establish the ultimate restaurant guide.

For the record, it started out as a simple guide for families who went out in their cars to eat at the weekend.

It was first published in 1900 by Andre and Edouard Michelin, owners of the French car tyre company of the same name.

At the beginning of the twentieth century, cars were scarce, and people believed they were only for short distances. For big excursions, they would go by train.

With the first guide, the Michelin brothers tried to change that. The guide contained information on gas stations, hotels, and car mechanics, as well as how to change a tyre. As time went on, maps and information about restaurants were included. But the restaurant section became increasingly more popular. The company then commissioned anonymous inspectors to evaluate the guide's hotels and restaurants.

In 1926, they introduced the star system. One star meant very good, two meant excellent cuisine and worth going out of your way for, and three meant incredible cuisine that justifies a trip of its own.

"It was a promise that you and your family would go out to eat with complete safety. This was the brand promise. Today, the Michelin guide is sold in 24 countries. So far, 30 million copies have been sold, building an extremely strong profile for the company, which originally established itself in people's minds as a reliable manufacturer of quality tyres."

Work hard in silence, let success make the noise.

Frank Ocean

Be Modest and Humble ... You Are Not Google

In 1984, President Reagan once again asked for the American vote to continue his work. His opponent is the leader of the Democrats and former Vice President of the USA, Walter Mondale. Mondale's campaign was based on the President's lack of physical strength and endurance, due to his old age.

In the debate, Reagan was asked about the issue by a journalist.

"Mr President, I would like to talk to you about the subject highlighted by the opposition for the last three weeks, namely that you are already the oldest President in the history of America. You looked very tired after the last confrontation with Mr Mondale, and the position often requires the President to be vigilant 24 hours a day. Is there any doubt in your mind that you'll be able to cope with such needs?"

His response was eloquently put.

"Mr Truitt, I want to make it clear to you and to those who are watching that I'm not going to make age the main subject of this campaign. I would never take advantage of the youth and lack of experience of my opponent."

That was it! Everyone laughed and the debate continued. So did Reagan's second term.

So, the message is simple. You are the founder of a start-up. Your company is not perfect. Very often, you don't even meet the basic criteria large companies have for their suppliers.

So, it's better to refer to your imperfections from the start.

By doing so, you will achieve three things:

First. The customer knows you aren't hiding anything from them. Therefore, you are honest and trustworthy.

Second. You do not come across as arrogant.

Third. You hide the bigger imperfections that probably exist.

Even big companies do this.

"I started the company 15 years ago from my room at home. The house didn't have powerful enough electricity. We had four employees and four servers powered by a single extension lead from a socket in the house. No one else in the house could plug in anything without tripping a fuse. We couldn't vacuum or switch on the cooker. The system would collapse. We had to leave the house and find an office. But things were moving very quickly.

"My 'favorite' mistake with our software was allowing our customers to order a negative number of books. So, if someone placed a negative order, we put money in their account as if we were buying it from them. We soon corrected it! Otherwise, we wouldn't be here today.

"It wasn't the only mistake. There were many like that! We've suffered many such wounds and injuries.

"At first, we set up a bell to ring whenever we received an order. Preparing to ship the order was amazing. Initially, it was always a member of the family. I remember the first time the bell rang from a regular customer, and we gathered around the table and asked each other whose mom it was . . .

"I'm happy to say that 30 days later, we removed the bell because it had become annoying."

This is Jeff Bezos, the founder of Amazon. The above is an extract from an interview he gave 10 years ago when Amazon was a big company, and not one of the largest capital-related companies in the world. If the richest man in the world can buckle like this in public, you can certainly do the same.

Remember, we're talking about the man who founded a company worth billions in a time before 'unicorns' came into fashion.

Nowadays, new potential unicorns appear every day. It's now become acceptable to promise the most and deliver the least, without fear and passion. In fact, companies like these are a long way from the guarantee of continued success investors are looking for, let alone survival.

There are countless examples of failed unicorns. Some of them got huge publicity, climbed to the highest pedestal of business fame but proved to be failures or even scams.

Given the rapid development of technology, there is a general pervasive tendency to exaggerate. Therefore, the message is to promise a little less than you can give and not confuse your customers or investors while trying to convince them of the value of your company and product.

 Remember that ego kills talent. Be modest and humble.

Steph Curry
Captain of the Golden State Warriors

One of the best advertisements of all time is the Avis car rental company campaign in 1964. Having failed to surpass its rival Hertz, the undisputed market leader at the time, it launched an ad that said:

'Avis is the No. 2 car rental company. So why come to us?'

And the answer was:

'We try harder.'

So, what did they do? They acknowledged their weakness and accepted second place while making a promise:

'We try harder!'

The same advertiser, the legendary Bill Bernbach, also designed the campaign for the launch of the Volkswagen 'beetle' on the American market. It was a huge challenge. The Americans, excited about huge American-produced cars, had no reason to buy a small, cheap, ugly, foreign car, which happened to be connected to Hitler.

This was during the late 1950s, and memories of World War II were still fresh.

The 'Think small' advertising campaign was voted the best advert of the twentieth century.

Why?

Because it took a disadvantage and turned it into an advantage. It was upfront and expressed another point of view.

Its opponents were out of arguments!

David Angelo, president of the David and Goliath advertising company, says, "If companies had the courage to show their weaknesses, the public could forgive mistakes and omissions much more easily. I believe that if people see authenticity, they recognize it and particularly appreciate it. That's when customers become ambassadors of your products."

So, this is the one thing that you should definitely do. When you make a mistake, acknowledge it. And do what you can to fix it.

Unless your name is Google, stop acting like you know everything.

Anonymous

"The luxury clock in the hotel said 2.35 a.m. The alarm went off with a bang. She got up without knowing what was going on around her.

"'Where am I? Oh . . . yes. In Singapore.'

"Probably a false alarm, she thought.

"'But I'm at the Ritz Carlton. They don't make mistakes here.'

"She put on her expensive bathrobe and walked down the stairs from the 13th floor. It was just a false alarm after all.

"'Even the Ritz Carlton makes mistakes!' she thought.

"In the morning, the whole thing felt like a dream. Did it really happen? The note under the door answered the question. A sincere apology, signed by Anne Lai, the hotel's sales manager, awaited all the guests at the Ritz.

"'She must have been awake all night,' she thought.

"That afternoon, after meetings at company headquarters, a bowl of fresh strawberries awaited her as compensation for the previous night's inconvenience. She could think of dozens of companies with endless experience of failures and yet the Ritz Carlton, where mistakes never happen, set the example of how to deal with them.

"'And how in the world did they know I like strawberries?'"

Mistakes and the ability to correct them allow the salesperson to show quality and caliber. If nothing else, the salesperson has the undivided attention of the customer in such cases. This experience is crucial and could be forever engraved in their memory.

You can keep a customer for many years if you handle a situation properly. It's a great opportunity. If the solution given was fair, timely and free of red tape, the customer will remember it forever.

I talk about this with Michael Virardi, who is a speaker, educator, and writer. Michael has given seminars and talks in 19 countries and some of the largest companies in the world, such as Google, Microsoft, Bayer, McDonald's, Ericsson, and many others. He mentioned something in particular.

"Strange as it may sound, making a professional mistake can be a miracle!

"Your own corrective actions after the mistake, such as an apology call or the immediate replacement of the product at no extra charge, are enough to turn a customer's negative attitude and experience into a positive one.

"According to the law of reciprocity (reciprocity principle) but also to human nature itself, when you make a mistake and correct it immediately, the person on the receiving end of the mistake feels obligated to you and reciprocates the obligation with his trust. In the business world, there's a good chance this customer will become a fan because they appreciate the recovery, the honesty but also the courage with which you handled the issue.

"According to the authors of the book *A Complaint is a Gift*, for every complaint we get from a customer, 26 others never reach us. That means about 96% of a company's customers don't voice their complaints and simply buy from the competitor. The good news is that 54–70% return to the same company for new purchases if their complaint is acknowledged and a further 95% will buy again if their request is settled immediately."

And he ended by saying, "Good companies differentiate from bad ones by the way they handle their mistakes, not by whether they make mistakes."

❝ Success depends on previous preparation, and without such preparation, there is sure to be failure.

Confucius

Be Prepared

On June 6, 1944, the landing that was intended to decide the outcome of World War II took place. The Allied Forces under the command of US General Dwight D. Eisenhower landed on the French coast, and the Normandy landings went down in history.

The armies were ready but hindered by bad weather and rough seas. German meteorologists assured General Rommel that for at least 12 days, the weather would be dire, and any military operation would be impossible.

On the other hand, American and British meteorologists told Eisenhower about a short, five-hour break in the bad weather at dawn on June 6, 1944.

Eisenhower landed in this short pause of bad weather. The risk was huge. If the Allied meteorologists had been mistaken, World War II could have had a different outcome. 6,700 ships and more than 80 divisions could have been at the mercy of incredibly bad weather in the Atlantic Ocean. The operation involved more than three million people, out of which 240,000 were Allied ships' personnel.

Therefore, whoever has the right information is most likely to win the war. The quality of the information, to a large extent, decides the outcome of every battle. Whether it's in a war or a company meeting.

 Consistency is the king.

Anonymous

In a previous chapter, I mentioned talk2lift.

In 2013, we began promoting the product, starting with the Greek market. A market in which potential customers in the midst of a financial crisis couldn't even pay the utility bill for the maintenance of the elevator in their apartment building.

We soon realized we'd have to go directly to the global market if we really wanted to commercialize our product.

So, we arrange a meeting with one of the largest elevator companies in the world, in Finland. Taking the prototype of talk2lift with us, we explored the possibility of immediate collaboration.

'In the worst-case scenario, we'll at least find out from the experts about how to improve our product,' we think.

The meeting is scheduled for 9.15 a.m. on a wintery Friday, just outside Helsinki. I get there the night before after flying via France, renting a car in Finland and arrive at a hotel near the meeting place at midnight.

I had one hour and 15 minutes at my disposal for the meeting the next morning. At 10.30 a.m., I had to leave the meeting to catch the first of a total of three return flights. I was flying from Helsinki to Copenhagen, from there to Munich, and would arrive in Thessaloniki just before midnight.

The total cost of the meeting with the Finnish company was approximately €750!

At the same time, a German competitor could take the morning flight and return the same day at noon for €51. He would also need a car for a few hours, maybe a meal. His total expenses would be around €125. For this reason, the central European supplier could repeat this trip once or twice a week, but for me, to repeat the trip at least once a month needed careful consideration.

My big mistake was to consider myself prepared. If I'd spent some time watching the latest news in Finland, I'd have acted differently. All the news bulletins showed Greece at its worst.

So, I was starting under terrible circumstances. There was no confidence in me, and the Greek origin of the product was a red flag.

If I'd known the situation, I could have handled it differently. Maybe I should have got these topics over and done with from the beginning of the discussion so there was more time for the essence of it. If I'd got some information from the Economic and Commercial Attaché at our Embassy there, or from Greek associations, my strategy would have been different.

 Knowledge is power.

Sir Francis Bacon

Preparation is the main weapon of all professionals, even athletes. I'd like to share with you the answer given by JaVale McGee, the LA Lakers Center at the time of writing, in an interview on an American internet radio station.

Talking about the championship he'd won with the Golden State Warriors and his all-star teammates, the conversation turned to Draymond Green, one of the greatest defenders in the NBA. He was asked what made him a superstar.

McGee said, "Draymond knows everything about the players he'll face in the game. Even the subs. He's studied the players and the teams to such an extent that every time a player is substituted, he tells the player marking him about the opponent's characteristics and what he should do to stop them.

"He even knows how the coaches move. I remember once he told me that if player X doesn't score the next three-pointer, they'll substitute him with a left-hander. If that guy loses the first two shots, he won't shoot again for the rest of the game, until he's replaced.

"Incredible preparation and hours of watching videos so he's ready every time to give his best."

So, before you meet with a potential client, do your homework, and read about anything you may have in common as well.

- Who are you about to meet?
- What are their interests? Where did they study? Do they smoke?
- What position do they hold in their company?
- Do they play tennis? Does their daughter go to dance class? What team do they support?
- Who else will be at the meeting? Who makes the decisions? Will they be there?
- If they won't, you may need to change the date of the meeting so they can be the next day.
- Look even deeper.
- What are they like in negotiations?
- What are they like with payments?
- See what happened lately in their company or the sector in general. It's good to be informed about these things too.
- Pay attention to timing. Is their job seasonal and you've caught them at their busiest? Has their company made any advance payments and will only get paid in six months? Or has the annual budget been finalized and you're only going for the P.R.?

Let's assume you've researched all of the above, initial communications have been made and the big meeting has been confirmed. You've noted all the key points of your presentation and you're ready to go.

The meeting will take place at their offices.

The next task is to learn about the venue.

Will you have access to the Internet? Do you need it?

Will you connect to a projector? Does the venue have a projector? Is there a TV? Does it take an HDMI cable, or do you need a VGA adapter?

Will you use your computer, or will you have to copy the presentation onto their computer?

What if you have a Mac? Will you be sharing images, or will you come up against firewalls that'll make your life difficult? Will your presentation have a video? And what about the sound? How does the volume go up and down? Do you operate it from your computer, or does it come from the projector, and do you need a remote control? Is there a console that emits sound from the speakers?

If you are not properly prepared, you'll waste time and look less professional than you really are.

Remember there are always solutions, as long as you know in advance that you'll have to deal with specific problems.

I recall a presentation I gave to investors in 2017. At the time, I was traveling once a week. During the day, I would give five presentations to potential clients and investors and usually returned on the evening flight. At one meeting, I arrived a few minutes before the scheduled time but my computer would not connect to the TV in the room. In an attempt to finish as quickly as possible with the equipment set up, I began to sweat.

When I eventually managed it, the meeting started 15 minutes late. The worst thing was that I was in an awkward position while presenting my presentation with sweat stains on my shirt. Not a particularly nice view . . .

 Either I will find a way, or I will make one.

Philip Sidney
Poet

I talked about the value of preparation with N.H., executive instructor in marketing, sales, and neurolinguistic programming. He told me how important it is for the salesperson to interact with sales conditions to increase the chances of success.

Having many years of experience in sales and training, N.H. knows exactly how to act in difficult situations. But that wasn't always the case. Despite his experience and countless hours of training, there were times when he, too, made tactical mistakes.

"I had a meeting with a potential client, owner of furniture stores. I remember entering his office and realising that the space was totally unsuitable to proceed with my presentation. The environment had a very negative effect, and it would not help me get my message across easily. There was a lot of noise, the phones were ringing, and they interrupted my co-speaker with irrelevant matters every now and then, which resulted in him losing his focus on the presentation. Normally, I should have stopped the presentation and repeated it some other time. I didn't, and at that stage, of course, I didn't manage to close the deal.

"Looking back, it's obvious I should have handled it differently. I should have stopped the presentation and explained like this:

"'Since it's very important you understand what I have to say, and the space and time are not helping, I'd like to request a new meeting so we can talk, and you can listen, and focus your attention on the appropriate answers to your questions.'

"The next presentation would have taken place in much more suitable conditions and I'd have been better able to explain why cooperation with them was so important."

A great presentation gives smart ideas an advantage.

Nancy Duarte,
Presentation Expert

Presentation

Some years ago, in Garland, Texas, a woman took her Siamese cat to the vet for its scheduled vaccination.

During the examination, the vet found something he didn't particularly like. The cat's balance was abnormal, and it could have been due to a tumor. The vet examined the cat from its tail right up to its head. Behind its right ear, he found a small pimple. He asked the cat's owner if he could perform a small operation and send the findings for biopsy. He went ahead and the tumor was found to be malignant. The cat was saved, thanks to the exceptional ability and professionalism of the veterinarian.

On the way out of the vet's, human behavior researchers asked the woman how she would score would the vet on that particular day.

Four hundred thousand customers in various businesses across Texas had been asked the same question.

She gave him a seven. Seven!

Why?

That day, the vet was wearing a shirt, a woolen sweater, jeans, and sneakers. His clothes were clean and quite expensive.

Research has shown that if a vet wears a blue lab coat, the average rating he gets from customers is 6.62.

If he had been wearing a white lab coat that day, he would have scored 7.35. And if he had been wearing a white lab coat with a stethoscope around his neck, his score would have been 8.82!

Why? Because we think with our eyes.

In the Selling the Invisible seminar, Christine Clifford says that if you are served terrible coffee anywhere in the world, in a fine porcelain cup on an embroidered tablecloth with Bocelli playing on the expensive sound system, the taste is unbeatable. Even if it's not!

Segesta was an ancient city in northwest Sicily. From 580 BC, it had had a poor relationship with Selinunte, the ancient Greek colony in the southwest of Sicily, which led to the Athenian-Sicilian Battle in 415 BC. When the Athenians arrived in Segesta to assess the situation, a false setting awaited them. A seemingly majestic temple clearly showed that Segesta was a rich city, a worthy candidate for an Athenian alliance.

A closer look revealed it was shoddily built, the columns were unfinished, there were no decorative colorful frescos, no roof, inner temple, or sanctuary.

To complete the setting, the Athenians were offered meals on gold plates with silver cutlery in various houses. What the Athenians didn't know was that they were the same dishes, hurriedly washed and taken from house to house to create a sense of wealth among its inhabitants.

They also offered to cover the expenses of the war, which they never did, as the Segestian reserves contained just 30 Talents, a minimal amount compared to the amount the Athenians expected the battle to cost.

The bluff worked! Athens, already caught up in the Peloponnesian Wars for 15 years, entered the Sicilian battlefield, dividing its forces. This was exploited by Sparta. This act marked the beginning of the end for the Athenians and their allies.

 Sellers who listen to buyers carefully and then give them the missing ingredients—those are the ones who stand out.

Deb Calvert

President of People First Productivity Solutions

We are visual beings. Visual aids help you tell bigger stories at the same time with the ability to receive more information much faster. The brain is designed to receive 400 to 500 words per minute, speaking at an average speed of 125 words per minute.

Vision is responsible for 85% of the information we receive. So, the largest part of the brain is reserved to receive visual information.

People remember 20% of what they hear, 30% of what they see, and 50% of the information they see and hear.

Communication is, therefore, almost three times more effective with visual aids.

This is also proven by statistics claiming that:

- 65% of people are visual types.
- 40% of people will respond better to visual information than plain text.
- 67% of people are more receptive to buying when they see graphics in a presentation.
- Color also helps a lot. Color catches the eye and enhances the expectation of an interesting presentation. Colored graphics increase people's desire to read content by 80%.
- Posts with images have 180% more participation.
- Percentages skyrocket with the use of video.
- Viewers are 85% more likely to buy a product after watching a product video.

The brain processes visual effects 60,000 times faster than text, and the time it takes to process visual sequences is only a quarter of a second. There is no doubt that visual narration is uniquely connected with nature and our psychology, as demonstrated by the history of visual arts, cinema, and television.

That is why visual storytelling has seen a significant increase in recent years and has become part of the daily life of consumers, through social networks, such as TikTok and

Instagram. Short videos, with compact content, are starting to prevail.

This is because they are mainly based on visual content since in most cases, the user watches them without sound.

 The success of your presentation will be judged not by the knowledge you send, but by what the listener receives.

Lilly Walters
Speaker

Talking about storytelling—even if I have devoted an entire chapter to that alone—I must emphasize how important it is to include a true customer story in your presentation—either your own or from the wider sector you are about to enter. This is how you grab the attention of the person in front of you by allowing him to identify as the consumer of your product.

When you do this, do not make the common mistakes that aspiring start-up founders usually make. Avoid complicated technical terms and long expressions. Use real names and realistic situations. Keep your story completely true.

Remember when people leave a presentation, they hold on to the stories that caught their attention.

And that was the reason you requested the meeting in the first place.

Ask yourself, 'If I only had sixty seconds on the stage, what would I absolutely have to say to get my message across?'

Jeff Dewar
Former Hockey Player

Y.K., the commercial director of Expert International in Switzerland says, "Successful, but also unsuccessful presentations, have specific characteristics."

So, I asked him to give me two examples from the countless presentations he has attended.

He said, "A successful presentation was the one that showed me a new way of approaching clients. It had never occurred to me that certain devices could be rented. It showed me a new way to approach consumers.

"In the presentation, the team had numbers, excellent communication skills and demonstrated that they knew the market very well. They were not afraid to admit to their mistakes, showing why they and other groups had previously failed to enter this market and why they would succeed now. Mainly, they demonstrated there was a market for this idea, especially for young people, particularly where technology products are involved.

"So, in the age of sharing economy, Millennials do not want to spend €1000 on a mobile phone. They prefer to spend €200 a year for three years and then exchange it for a newer model. The three-year-old mobile phone holds on to its value, of course, and can easily find a new owner at a lower price. This would greatly reduce the build-up of customers who have had the same smartphone for five years and don't buy a new one because of the high price. These people demonstrated that their idea covers a real gap in the market.

"On the other hand, an unsuccessful presentation was just the opposite. The potential associate came to the venue wearing jeans and a polo shirt. We were meeting this gentleman for the first time. He did not communicate openly; the whole presentation was about how big and great his company was and had nothing to do with Expert. He gave us information I had seen on the Internet while we were preparing for the meeting before he arrived. It was a presentation with the wrong setup and resulted in a fruitless meeting."

So, what are the characteristics of a successful presentation? And how many are there? Y.K. replied, "I would say five key things:

1. The presentation should be simple. An impressive slide that took you half an hour to set up to give a lot of information in a very busy setting is wrong. You lost me!
2. It must show who you are, what you have, and why what you have suits me and my needs.
3. It must not exceed 20 minutes. You need to know when to end the presentation. Do not waste someone else's time for no reason. Do not talk relentlessly. Bring the

presentation to a close at the right time and if you are given more time, continue with questions.

4. The day you make your first contact, you must be prepared. More specifically:

   a. Appropriate attire.

   b. Be on time. Call before the meeting to confirm the appointment. It shows professionalism.

   c. If, after the first contact, you promised you would call or send samples in five days, keep your word. There aren't that many opportunities to demonstrate your reliability. If anything changes, inform the customer in good time.

5. The aim of the first meeting is to secure a second. Don't forget that."

Make a customer, not a sale.

Katherine Barchetti

Sell It!

Imagine you are an airline passenger. After a long flight, you land in London and realize the plane has come to a standstill a long way from the terminal. You have to take the bus to get there. Your mood changes automatically. Then, the pilot switches on his microphone and makes the following announcement.

"We have arrived at our destination. Unfortunately, there are no free jetways."

If the announcement had stopped here, most passengers would have been disgruntled. The pilot continues.

"The good news is that you'll be picked up by a bus that goes straight to passport control, so you don't have to carry your luggage all that way."

What just happened?

The bus always went straight to passport control. Why was everyone suddenly happier? Is saying something differently enough?

You need to remember that all products, whether large or small, are simple or complex for one reason: To make the user feel better. To make their life more enjoyable, easier, exciting, happy. It's all related to the customer's self-image. How they feel about their image, their life, their ambitions, and their aspirations. And how your product will improve those and help them achieve the desired effect.

Sometimes, good and bad impressions are simple reflections of the mind in each situation. So, the answer to the above question is yes.

Sometimes, you just have to say it differently.

One day, a customer called an airline to buy a ticket from Los Angeles to New York. He wanted to be there in the morning, so had to travel all night. He asked if they had a red-eye flight. It's called that because after traveling all night, you turn up at your meeting with red eyes. The girl on the other end of the line said they didn't have those flights. The customer was worried.

"How can that be possible? There aren't any night flights to New York?"

The airline clerk replied, "Of course, there are. There's the Moonlight Special flight."

That is the exact same flight with better packaging. A tiring and arduous activity turned into a beautiful, adventurous one.

Value the relationship more than making your quota.

Jeff Gitomer
Author

Never start selling with features and benefits. Imagine that 30 people like you have already gone through a list of characteristics.

What the customer wants to hear is how this product will change their lives and how it will make them better. Which of their needs does it respond to? Usually, the customer is looking for the advantage that will make their life easier, change it, and take it up a level. The Americans say 'WIIFM—what's in it for me?'

Brian Tracy says that 15% of the customers buy for how it was before and 85% for how it will be after. What will they gain if they buy? So, if you're selling an excursion to the Canary Islands, just talk about how the customer will feel when they're relaxing on a deck chair on the beach. Don't tire yourself by saying what they will gain from you. Don't expect the customer to make a 'spiritual leap' to understand what you mean.

Nikolaos Dimitriadis, author of *Neuroscience for Leaders* agrees with the above. Nikolaos claims that the human brain tries to find a strategy that minimizes 'pain' and maximizes gain. It revises strategies and changes its approach every second. When you can prove the customer will go from 'pain' to gain, people react surprisingly.

So, always start with how to solve the customer's basic problem. Don't refer to the problems the customer you are addressing doesn't have. Then, if you have time, you can go on to a second. Always bear in mind that you usually won't have time to finish the presentation. So at least make sure you cover the basics.

Also, don't give multiple alternatives. The customer needs a few specific options. Otherwise, they won't buy.

In a supermarket in England, there were two open chillers selling jam. The customers could try the jam, choose the flavor they wanted from the machine, and fill any jar they liked. The first open chiller had six flavors and the second had 24. The first convinced 30% of customers to buy jam. However, only three percent of the customers were convinced by the second open chiller.

Procter and Gamble came to the same conclusion. A global firm that sells everything from laundry detergent to medication. One of its popular products is Head and Shoulders. When the company reduced its range of shampoos from 26 to 15, it soon saw a 10% increase in sales.

 You can't build a reputation on what you are going to do.

Henry Ford
Businessman

The best way to 'sell' in my opinion is to believe in it a lot. Because, if you believe in it, it shows in the way you talk about it. And if that's the case, you don't really need any training.

According to Grant Cardone, sales trainer and author, if you don't push the customer to close the deal with you, you neither believe in yourself, your product, nor your company.

"Faith means confidence in the truth. What truth? That this is a good product, and this is a good deal for your customer. So, you push someone into it if you're absolutely certain that with your product it will gain value, solve problems, and make life easier for them. If you promise all this and don't persuade the other person to conclude the deal with you, then you probably don't believe in it enough and are, therefore, unable to convince them."

In 1859, chemist Robert Chesebrough observed that when petrol was extracted, a slimy substance came out with it. Workers hated it because it immobilized the drills.

However, this substance also had beneficial properties, and when it came into contact with wounds and scratches, they healed much faster.

Ten years later, he created what he then called 'Petroleum Jelly'. A few years later, he renamed it 'Vaseline'.

The market was not impressed. The product did not sell as predicted. Then, Chesebrough began presenting the product. He burned his skin with acid or fire in public and smeared Vaseline over it to prove its healing properties. The scars, of course, would last forever. The presentations worked.

People started buying it in masses. In 1874, a jar of Vaseline was sold every minute! Consumers believed in the product because its manufacturer was prepared to hurt himself to prove its worth. He believed in it so much that he ate a spoonful of Vaseline every day to stay healthy. When he became seriously ill in his sixties, he asked a nurse to cover him in it and give him a spoonful of Vaseline every morning.

He reached the age of 96, ending a magical life.

Let's move on to a Greek who believed in something with all his heart. He believed in it so strongly that he thought he'd be able to make everyone follow his idea. Even when his life was in danger.

In 1907, the great poet Angelos Sikelianos met American Eva Palmer in Greece and married her in America.

In 1924, the couple settled in Delphi and began implementing the Delphic Idea. This was the rebirth of the Delphic Celebrations, a combination of ancient tragedy, Byzantine music and folk art, the cost of which would be covered by the wealthy Eva.

It should be noted that Delphi at the time was nothing like it is today. There were no roads or infrastructure.

Nevertheless, in May 1927, the first Delphic Festivals took place, and were a great success and attended by thousands of visitors from Greece and abroad.

In 1930, the second Delphic Festivals took place, with politicians in attendance and was equally as successful as the first. The rich American bride's money soon ran out and without help from the state, the big idea came to an end. The circumstances in which the Sikelianos' dream came true, however, are very interesting.

One day, a local shepherd approached the poet and gave him a misspelled note telling him he should wait at the fountain until midnight and have 10,000 drachmas with him. He also made it clear that if he did not go or warn others, he would kill him at the first opportunity. The note was signed by a notorious criminal of the time, called Monastiriotis.

At nightfall, Sikelianos went to the fountain and waited.

Monastiriotis, after making sure that Sikelianos was alone, approached and asked for the money. Sikelianos replied that he did not bring any money and that he simply wanted to meet him. He said, "Everyone says you are a vicious beast and I do not believe it. I imagined you to be valiant, and I came to meet you."

Monastiriotis was astounded and asked him if he did not bring the ransom money with him was because he didn't have the money.

"I have what you asked for and much more. But for my work to succeed, I need even more," he answered.

The thief asked what kind of work required so much money.

Sikelianos began to narrate his dream and why it was so important to bring the Delphic Idea to life. Monastiriotis lowered his rifle and listened until morning. He also offered him a melon from his bag and when he left, and said,

"I want to come to the festival, Mr Angelos, but how can I, dressed in these rags, unshaved and unkempt? I will remain faithful to the idea, however."

In 1950, after many years of trying, the Greek poet managed to obtain a financial grant for the revival of the Delphic Festivals. On June 19, 1951, Angelos Sikelianos died and was buried in Delphi.

" Negotiation is the art and science of getting what you want.

Anonymous

Rule No. 19

Negotiations

In 2013, a few months before talk2lift was launched on the market, we scheduled a meeting to present the product at a large European elevator manufacturer. The meeting took place at a very high level. The owners, the Chief Executive Officer and the Commercial Director, were present.

During the presentation, they showed interest but also doubted whether we could deliver a technologically advanced solution that was a global innovation. At the end of the talk2lift demo, the CEO of the company took the floor and said, "Gentlemen, this is what we suggest. Develop the product at your own expense and when you're done, give us 20% free of charge. We'll install them in elevators in various parts of Europe and if we like them, we'll buy them exclusively from you at a price set by us."

I got up from my seat, thanked the host company for the meeting and left, saying I was used to being treated respectfully at such meetings. Maybe I wasn't that polite.

For a long time, I thought that maybe I should have handled the matter differently. Maybe I should have been more accommodating and explored other ways of collaboration and other alternatives.

I told Chris M., human resources development consultant, about it. Chris has been teaching negotiation for the last 15 years. While negotiating, he considers it important to be well prepared, know your product, and the competition well, know the problems that require solutions, and exactly what you need for sales. He told me, "The more time you devote to building trust and understanding the person's job so you can act as a consultant to solve their problem, the less you will need in the end to handle the client's arguments.

"The more time you devote to the previous steps, the less you will need to close the deal, i.e., to respond to objections.

"So, if you've spent enough time on the sale, you'll need minimal time for the negotiations."

Negotiations and sales are perfectly interconnected concepts. They go together. They are not however the same thing. Selling is a process by which you are trying to persuade a client to buy what you have. Negotiation aims at establishing the details of the agreement.

As a start-up, your negotiating capacity is limited.

Usually, you're trying to convince the client about something innovative. Sometimes, you will have to prove you are solving a problem they are yet unaware of with a product they have never used before and requires training. Which, of course, they don't want.

In a raid in Seattle, USA, the police cornered a serial killer. The killer had taken two hostages.

The local police negotiator, who was more active than usual, set to work. The kidnapper turned around and said, "You're not doing your job very well, dude. Now is the time to build communication. Read the manual."

In negotiations, therefore, you are almost always up against a business executive who has been in the same position many times before and knows the subject well. Better than you.

Mostly though, they know they generally have the upper hand.

Returning to my own case, according to Chris, it would have been useful if I had visualized the subject earlier and was prepared for every possibility. I should have thought about what could go wrong, who could spoil things, which questions could have complicated the situation, and what the correct answers were. Also, what an ideal agreement looked like.

Finally, I had to find a way to leave the door open.

"Never close the door," he said.

Looking back, I realize that it was a mistake to try and close a deal at the first meeting.

When they made me such a terrible offer, maybe I could have broken it down and analyzed their individual needs and attitudes. If we had some common ground, maybe the discussion would have gone better. According to Chris, negotiation has seven steps, the last of which is the most important.

"Comply with what has been agreed. The way the conversation started, even if a channel of communication had been developed, the agreement would probably not have been kept by the other side."

The seven steps are:
1. Introduction
2. Initial positions
3. Concessions
4. Variables and alternatives
5. Central agreement
6. The agreement must be a win-win so that the relationship is long-lasting
7. Comply with what has been agreed

For the record, I must mention that the collaboration finally went ahead when the CEO left the company on bad terms two years later, and the company called us back after seeing our product on a TV show.

Expect the best. Prepare for the worst. Capitalize on what comes.

Zig Ziglar
Writer and Sales Trainer

Negotiation is a huge and specific area. But even here, there are basic rules you can follow. Even as a start-up founder.

Negotiations are like public speaking, speaking in front of an audience. The solution is preparation. Do the work here, too. Think about what you can give, about who you are talking to, what's important to them, what their habits are, how they pay, what they are looking for, and in what way.

So, you have to be very well prepared. You may know your product well, but if you don't have a negotiation strategy, it could cost you a lot. Much more than the cost of the time you'd need to invest to prepare properly. It's also a very good idea to listen in negotiations and gather information about the other side that you couldn't find while preparing.

Make sure you are prepared for various situations while negotiating—even modifications while it's taking place. Know when to back off and when you should postpone.

Like in sales, the negotiating process goes much better if there is trust and common points of interest.

When you visualize the negotiation in your mind, calculate its beginning, middle and end. It's like a book. You also need to know when to start the conclusion.

The best negotiation is the one that results in a win-win situation because you could get a good deal for yourself that could prove to be bad for the other side. At the same time, your collaboration will certainly be short. If you think it costs you time and money to win over every customer, while existing customers only require your presence, you'll realize that a short-term relationship is of no use to you either in the medium or long term.

Try to configure the collaboration package with the client. Your main goal is to avoid being on the opposite side of a table where one of you wins and the other loses. It's good to be on the same side, trying to solve a common problem. Once your partner has helped you develop a good solution, they will likely accept that solution without a second thought.

Do not show weakness. If you let it show that you really need this deal, and if you close it, it will be on the worst possible terms for you. When it comes down to price, which is very common, you have to take the time to ask questions. Explore the possibility of offering them something else for added value.

Never quote a better price straightaway. But in case you must, look to get something in return. If you make concessions without consideration, the other party will think they can ask for more without paying.

So, if it requires a lower price, ask for a larger order or even a larger deposit. And each time, justify it:

'To give you this, you have to give me that, because I have to justify it to other customers, partners, etc.'

Some argue that it's better to give something away first to set the tone of the negotiation. If you need to give up something from the beginning—maybe even before the meeting—to get the other side in a good mood at the negotiating table, give up things that don't mean much to you.

If the negotiation is not going well, take a time-out. When the target becomes distant and everyone needs a breather, take a break. Many deals were saved by a break at the right time. Use the break to get closer. Talk about things that unite you outside of work: football, holidays, family, children, etc.

In the book by Roger Fisher and William Ury, *Getting to YES*, the authors say that to avoid bitter and lengthy negotiations, you must rely on three basic principles:

First, put yourself in their position and look at the agreement from their side.

To accomplish this, it's a good idea to say after their initial positions:

'Allow me to try and summarize your position.'

Describe the reasoning behind the other person's position.

For example, in a situation where an employee requests a pay raise from his or her team leader, the supervisor could summarize as follows:

'From what I understand, you're asking for a an increase of 5% than the rest because you achieved all last year's goals and have undertaken more difficult tasks than those of your associates, right?'

Here, you achieve three things.

First, the 'opposition' feels that you listened to them and understood their specific issue in the negotiation.

In addition, you may realize that what you are being asked for is not as above the limit as you initially thought. You may succeed when the other person realizes they are asking for too much and should step back.

Finally, by exchanging views and developing communication, it's much more likely you'll end up on the same side of the table trying to solve the problem.

Second, go for a win-win situation. Often, a negotiation can be finalized with both parties getting what they want because they end up pursuing different things.

If, as CEO of your start-up, you're interested in keeping costs low and your employee wants higher pay, but believes in the company a lot, there's a way you can both be satisfied. You keep his salary at the same level and the employee gets shares in the company, which will make it worth their while in the future. In this way, the employee feels they are being paid appropriately and will also benefit if the company does better.

Third, insist on the use of objective criteria. Let's say you crashed your car and the insurance refuses to pay the required amount for the damage. If you decide to go to court, what would you do? You would probably search for information about the value of the car from reputable sites and magazines, and get offers from garages. A lawyer would be more likely to win this lawsuit.

If you take the lawyer and the court out of the equation by presenting objective evidence to the other side, you can lead a bad negotiation to a good result for you.

 Learn the rules like a pro, so you can break them like an artist.

Pablo Picasso
Artist

Continuing the conversation with Chris M., I asked him to think back over the years and tell me about a negotiation that went quite well and one that ended badly.

"In 1996, we had a meeting with Olympic Airways. The company was in a strange situation at the time but Olympic always had funds for training. We already knew that. So, we began with the positive aspects.

"The CEO of the company at the time was well-informed, as he used to teach Aviation Management in England and was a consultant for British Airways.

"He also had a clear view of the subject and the training method we were proposing. He asked the Human Resources Officer if they had the necessary funds to cover our proposal which amounted to $\mathcal{D}_p$70 million, quite a large sum of money for the time.

"The answer was negative. The CEO said there was no point in discussing it further.

"I said if he'd allow me to explain the return he would get and the reduction in costs it would bring, he might change his mind. So, I submitted detailed financial data—because we were very well prepared—and proved that with some management changes and a combination of actions achieved as a result of the training, there would be a serious reduction in costs.

"He turned to his executives and asked if what I'd just said was true. When he received a positive answer, the CEO, who was not easy to negotiate with, put the following proposal on the table. The $Dp70$ million would be broken down into three parts. The first part, about $Dp30$ million, would cover the fee.

"For the second package of $Dp25$ million, he introduced a variable we were not able to influence. He said we wouldn't be paid if less than 15 people attended each seminar. And the remaining $Dp15$ million would be paid in the form of Olympic Airways tickets.

"So, the total amount was within his initial budget and the profit would be at least one hundred million.

"Two years later, he wrote to us saying that Olympic Airways' profit, in terms of cost reduction, was well above the one hundred million he was expecting. So, this was a clear win-win situation.

"On the other hand, I remember a case where we might have been luckier if we had prepared better. In the late 1990s, we made an offer to the CEO of Mega (TV) Channel for an internal evaluation survey and a staff training program. The channel had a human resources department at the time and was very well organized.

"We gave the presentation which demonstrated that improving the intangible potential would also increase the channel's audience. They showed a lot of interest because what we were saying was well substantiated and the channel needed better ratings at the time, especially at prime time.

"But we had failed to consider that it wasn't just the management in control; the journalists played a major role in the decision-making, too.

"The journalists saw it as an internal undercover operation to evaluate them and decided they wouldn't take part in the procedures and training. They sabotaged the program before it even started, and we were never able to implement it.

"What we could have done differently was understand the situation better, know everyone's role in the negotiation and the power each of them had. If we had done this, we'd have talked to everyone involved in advance to prepare the ground before entering the game."

To close this chapter, I asked Chris to give me five basic tips he would give to a start-up founder entering a negotiation. He suggested the following:

1. The person who does the most damage is you on a bad day.
2. Always be prepared.

3. A meeting is never wasted. Even if you don't close a deal, try to get information about the competition and the market.

4. There are certain steps to negotiate and it isn't over in one go. So, don't rush it.

5. Never close the doors. Don't take things personally. The marketplace is a live entity and changes constantly. Maybe the opportunity will present itself again when something goes wrong with a company that chose the competition. If you made a wrong move, they'll look for another solution.

 Show me the money!

Jerry Maguire,
The movie

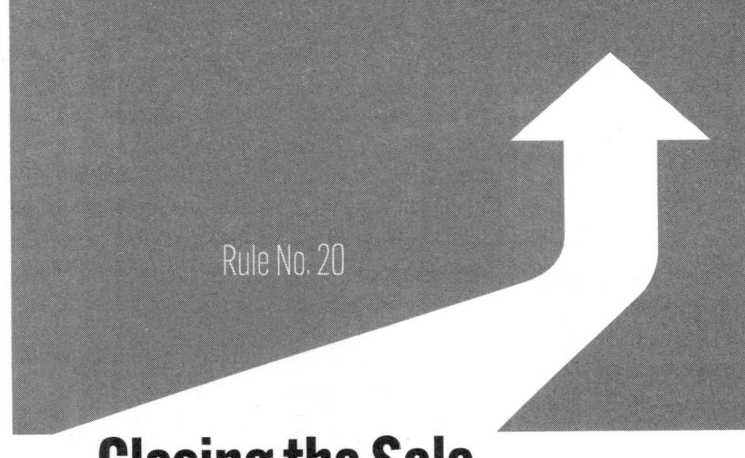

Closing the Sale

"The first tuxedo I bought was sold to me by a gentleman I had gone to, intending to rent. He took a brand-new tux out of the warehouse and started marking it. I told him I wanted to rent it for a wedding, but he said not to worry because he wanted to have a new one available for rent in my size.

"He must have understood me very well because I felt comfortable wearing a brand-new tuxedo, which was exactly my size and at the rental price. When it was ready and I went to pick it up, I tried it on again to make sure it was OK. He gave me a shirt, a belt, and a bow tie to wear. The whole outfit looked amazing.

"Guess what happened next? He asked me how many children I had and how many there are in my extended family. And before I knew it, he 'proved' that with so many weddings coming up in the future, it would be more profitable to buy this tuxedo made of mohair and silk, which 'actually fits like a glove', than to rent it every time.

"What the tailor said turned out to be true. Looking back, I think that even if I didn't save money, buying it saved me from rushing to rent a tuxedo every time I had a wedding or an event to go to."

This story was narrated by Joe Girard, the best salesman in the world, according to the Guinness Book of Records.

> If you're not moving closer to what you want in sales, you probably aren't doing enough asking.

Jack Canfield
Author

Selling is an art. If artists find it difficult to finish a work of art, the same happens with a salesperson while closing a sale or a deal. Why? Because the customer can back off, even at the last minute.

Most people act defensively in the presence of a salesperson. They see them as someone who wants to shift money out of their wallet into their own.

Fear of making the wrong choice and losing money is

greater than the fear of losing out on an opportunity. So, it's easier for the customer to say no.

They react defensively or escape. Everyone measures themselves in terms of 'pain'. How much something will 'hurt' them if they don't have it. They put themself in the worst situation they can imagine. The pain stimulus deals with it and alleviates it, so they don't hurt anymore.

The brain only has two stimulus networks: approach or avoidance.

What does avoidance mean? We avoid bad feelings, sadness, or deep disappointment. This is a message to do something to return to a neutral state. On the other hand, approach means gain. If you don't have it, you're fine, but if you do, you think you're the best version of yourself. By the way, avoidance is twice as powerful as an approach. That's why we encounter it the most.

Research has shown that customers do not buy for seven reasons.

1. *I don't need it.*
    People don't always buy what they need. If they did, we wouldn't be the over-consuming society we are today. So, you sell what people want.

2. *I don't want it.*
    The customer would usually say, "I'm not in the mood for it." This is the most difficult category.

3. *I haven't got the money.*
    Nobody wants to be in debt. They'll only go that far if what they're buying will help them either make money or improve their life or alleviate some of their 'pain'. If your product does not do any of these three, it's time to leave.

4. *I don't think it's worth the price.*
    Here, the right answer comes from the legendary Tom Hopkins, a distinguished salesman and author of the bestseller *How to Master the Art of Selling*.

    I've learned something over the years, you know. When people spend money, they want three things: the best quality, the best service, and the lowest price. I know that no company can offer all three. No one can offer the best quality and the best service at the lowest price. So, for your own benefit, which of the three would you be willing to sacrifice in the long run? Good quality, excellent service, or the lowest price?

5. *I don't trust the salesperson.*
    Why not? Because they've been deceived in the past. So as a rule, they doubt the real impact your product will have on their lives. The best way to dispel this fear is to make a list of satisfied customers who would be willing to receive a phone call from the potential customer.
    A UK electronics chain has its employees call customers five days after they've made a purchase to find out if everything went well with delivery and installation and if the device works okay.

Immediately after—if the answers they received were the desired ones—they ask the customers if they would be willing to accept a phone call from someone considering buying the same device. Sixty percent of them answer negatively but the 40% who answer positively make for an easy sale to new customers because while a customer may be wary of a salesperson, he or she is particularly open to someone who was in the same position as them a few days ago.

6. *I am afraid I am committing an error.*
    Here again, a lot of questions are required. They must trust you. It's logical! You are a start-up, and they're a company executive. Every high-risk decision must be accompanied by an appropriate incentive. So, you need to know what you're offering extremely well to prove the added value of your offer.

7. *I don't quite understand the product I'm buying.*
    In this case, the customer simply postpones by saying, "Why close the deal now and not in six months?"

The answer, in this case, is that I could have had children 10 years later, but I'd have been in my forties, not my thirties, and under different circumstances, would have had less stamina. I could have bought my house 15 years later, when my finances were better but then, I'd have been 50 years old and wouldn't have enjoyed it like I have been doing for the last 15 years. 'Later' is always more convenient in the mind of the customer.

But what you lose in the meantime needs to be factored in. Don't waste time.

 If you're not gonna go all the way, why go at all?

Joe Namath
Actor

Some say it takes a lot of small things to make a deal. People like Chris Voss, writer and speaker, say, "Go along with 'no' until you get a 'that's it!'"

In the 1980 US election, Governor Ronald Reagan debated with President Carter and followed the following strategy precisely.

"Are you better off than four years ago? Do your children go to better schools? Does the state give you better services? Do you pay less taxes? Are you happier than four years ago? If so, vote for Carter again."

The election was won by the candidate who got consecutive negative answers until the 'that's it!'

That's when you close the deal.

Zig Ziglar is a writer, speaker and one of the best sellers and sales trainers in the world. He was born in 1926, in Alabama, USA. By the end of his career, he had written 30 books and held countless seminars and speeches.

But things were not always that easy. When he started out

selling kitchenware door to door, 'no' was the only answer he ever got.

His first book, *See You at the Top*, was rejected 39 times until it was finally published in 1975, and it is still in print today. Along the way, he managed to evolve and reach a good standard of living.

In one of his books, *Secrets of Closing the Sale*, he says that selling and closing are not mysteries to be solved. Instead, they are as tangible as when his wife sold him on a new house.

 Selling without closing is just conversation.

Anonymous

The Ziglar family, with four children, managed to get out of the hotel they were living in and rented a small house. One day, his wife Jane asked him if he would be willing to buy a house, 'now that prices are still low.'

Zig said it was too early and that they'd have to wait for work to improve before making a move. Jane, however, had her reasons.

"You're always away. The children never see you. If we had space for an office at home, you'd be here more, and you wouldn't miss out on the best years of their lives. On the other hand, look at it as an investment. Everyone says prices will rise in the years to come. If work doesn't go well, we'll sell the house for a profit and rent again."

The future sales trainer realized he had a lot to learn from his wife. He agreed to an initial search, which would proceed to a purchase, only if they found the house they wanted for the money they had. But how much was that?

Ziglar said that to be worthy of his obligations to the bank, the amount should not exceed $120,000. His wife said, "Hypothetically speaking, if we did find the house of our dreams, and if it would meet all our current and future needs as a family, by how much could we exceed that amount?"

He felt he was falling into a trap and there was no way out.

"I don't want to exceed that amount," he said. "If we were to find our dream home, at the best price in the history of real estate in America, we could exceed the initial amount by $20,000."

So, Jane began the search and one afternoon, made an announcement.

"I've found a house I'd like you to look at. The agent is expecting us."

"How much?" Ziglar asked.

"$158,000," she replied. "We don't need to buy it. I just want you to take a look at it so you can see what I think would meet our needs. So, if we find a house like it for the money we have, we'll keep the initial agreement."

The estate agent showed the couple the house, listing all its strong points. Zig signaled indifference, ruling out a further increase in the amount he was willing to spend. The house was amazing and well worth the money.

The final discussion took place that evening.

"Yes, I agree. The house is amazing. But I can't pay for it. It's out of my budget."

"Yes," replied his wife, "by $18,000."

Here, I have to point out that the original amount of $120,000 was not even mentioned. It no longer existed.

Each negotiation started with the highest amount the previous one stopped at. That's where the statements demanding a small, silent 'yes' began. The conversation ended with a big question, with an emphatic 'yes' even if no one said it.

"The amount we'd be borrowing from the bank would be $18,000 more. The loan will be for 30 years. So, that will be $600 a year, $50 a month. That's $1.67 a day. So, you're saying that making your wife happy is not worth $1.67 a day?"

I think we all know what happened next.

When you've closed a sale, stay in touch. It doesn't end there.

Amanda Johns Vaden,
Author

After the Sale

You closed the deal. Congratulations! Now what? What do you do next? It's time to get serious about customer service. You didn't care about that until now because you had no customers. But now you do.

And you should keep them happy for two main reasons:

First, gaining a new customer costs six to eight times more than retaining an existing one. It's, therefore, beneficial to keep your customer happy.

Second, the recommendations.

Let's take a look.

I talked to S.T., an entrepreneur who, after various jobs, was hired by the sales department of a cable TV channel. After that, he worked as a Western Union salesman for three and a half years and left in 2002, after gaining experience in money transfer. Six months later, MoneyGram approached him and offered him a job, suggesting he become their representative for Italy, Greece, and Cyprus.

> "I went to London for the initial discussions and found out that a Greek partner was already delivering on the pre-arranged agreement. I told them I'm interested in running the project and they gave me a license and the go-ahead straightaway.
>
> "I started in 2003. At first, it was difficult. You could say it was just like a start-up for me because I was on my own, up against a multinational company with satisfied customers. The following year, I was hospitalized twice due to stress.
>
> "From 2005 onwards, the company began making a profit. In 2010, I started my second company, a payment institution. MoneyGlob met needs in countries where MoneyGram couldn't or didn't want to. Bangladesh, Lebanon, and other countries that are difficult to approach on the subject were best for me. They work without intermediates and profit per transfer was much higher than with the American multinational.
>
> "From 2011 to 2013, my own payment institution grew substantially, and MoneyGram bought me out and I made a successful exit!"

Looking back, he believes the biggest lesson he learned was when he was hired by NOVA Customer Service. He remembers this in particular:

> "It was here I realized that the Customer Service Department is the image of the company to the outside world. This image must be kept flawless. The sale always comes first. But from the moment you make a sale, customer service is the ultimate tool to retain the customer and gain the next one. As far as I'm concerned, a company can't exist without this."

 Sales go up and down. Service stays forever.

Anonymous

So, as a start-up founder without the relevant experience, there are specific steps to follow. Your team must get together and ask all the possible questions a customer would ask and answer them in the best possible way.

You should also finalize what those who answer the phone calls should say if they don't know the answer to a question. The customer doesn't want to hear them lingering for no reason. So, replies must be clear and specific even if the answer is unknown.

Rest assured, even large corporate customer service departments are unable to give a definite answer when asked at the end of the year about the five biggest and most common problems they had to deal with.

At start-up level, however, this should be made clear because these are the problems that will also determine the changes that need to be made to the product. And it's the best information you can get about the market. Comments, therefore, should be recorded and conveyed to the people who design the product.

Zappos has become a legendary company for its exemplary customer service. It's a very successful website that sells shoes online. The company has taken the matter to another level. It made calls longer than 10 hours. One of their customers wanted to order pizza and the Zappos employee thought it was 'cool' and did so. A woman found out after her mother's death that she was addicted to buying shoes when she found hundreds of unworn pairs in her wardrobe. Zappos took them all back without a second thought.

In his book, *Delivering Happiness*, Zappos CEO Tony Hsieh outlines 10 ways to build the ultimate customer service philosophy in your company:

1. Make customer service a priority for the whole company. Not just for the department.
2. The right attitude toward customer service must be demonstrated by the leadership.
3. Empower and trust your people in customer service.
4. Understand that 'firing' customers often has to be done.
5. Do not time the duration of calls and do not record conversations.
6. Set up a free communication line.
7. Think of each call as an investment that will build your

reputation for good service and not as an expense that should be reduced.

8. Get the whole company to celebrate good service by sharing colleagues' stories of excellent customer care.
9. Find and hire people who are already enthusiastic about communication and customer service.
10. Offer excellent service to all. Customers, suppliers, and employees.

This culture is the main reason for the company's success and was reflected by its acquisition by Amazon, for $1.2 billion in 2009.

 Your most unhappy customers are your greatest source of learning.

Bill Gates

In the book *Connected*, Nicholas Christakis and James Fowler refer to the six degrees of separation or better said, the distance between six people. According to the authors (although the conception of the idea was originally expressed by Frigyes Karinthy in 1929), everyone on earth is separated by six at the most social connections, especially in friend-to-friend relationships. It has also been observed that a friend's friend affects you even if you have never met them.

It's obvious that combining the aforementioned information with the interaction of human networks makes recommendations even more important.

Joe Girard, 'the best salesman in the world' according to the Guinness Book of Records, reminds us that after the conclusion of a deal, the sale continues. As a car salesman in America, he kept in touch with all his customers by giving gifts of food and drinks, and offering a reward for every customer they sent him. He sent them birthday cards (in the pre-internet and Facebook era) called them a month after they had bought the car to offer a free technical inspection, and much more.

As a result, he received recommendations from his existing customers and also had the same customer lined up to sell him a car again when five or six years later, he wanted a replacement.

He said that every customer, everybody, has a circle of two hundred and 50 friends. He deduced this when he noticed that at every wedding or funeral he attended, the same number of people were present.

"So, do you want some dissatisfied guy telling another 250 people how bad a salesman you are, or would you prefer to advertise to the same people for next to nothing? The decision is yours."

If I still haven't managed to convince you that referrals are one of the easiest ways to get new customers, consider the following: when a colleague, partner or friend of a potential client recommends you, you immediately gain the same level of trust as the person who is recommending you. So, you've already taken the first important steps without wasting your time, or of your client.

In fact, if you've managed to get a mutual friend to talk about your product, the other person subconsciously creates a feeling of recognized value and quality in what you are offering, and is also able to trust you.

Always remember it's much easier to get recommendations from someone who has recommended you before than from someone who hasn't. But never forget to tell them about how it went and thank them. Only then can you ask for a recommendation again.

In 1706, Benjamin Franklin was born in America. A great politician, but also an inventor, diplomat, and writer, he was multifaceted in general. But until he gained the respect and recognition of all, there was much great rivalry and dislike. On the other hand, he also had the reputation of a man who overcame obstacles by using tools of persuasion, unknown to most people even today!

At one point, shortly before the War of Independence, in which he played a key role securing the French alliance against the British, he was particularly troubled by the intense political rivalry of a prominent Pennsylvania executive and member of the senate.

He knew his political opponent had a large library of excellent books, including a very rare edition. He wrote to the owner, asking him to lend it to him for a few days.

He received the book, read it, and returned it within the promised time, accompanied by a letter thanking its owner and acknowledging the favor.

After that, everything changed. The attitude of his opponent was no longer one of hatred, but the opposite, one might say. The man repeatedly offered his services to Franklin until the day he died.

> Statistics suggest that when customers complain, business owners and managers ought to get excited about it. The complaining customer represents a huge opportunity for more business.

Zig Ziglar
Writer and Sales Trainer

The easiest way to sell to someone is for that person to value you. Get on with them as a person and like them. Eighty-five percent of recommendations come from such people.

According to the Sandler Method, the four ways a customer can make a recommendation are:

1. *The cold referral.* Your customer gives you a phone number and a name. Success rates here amount to 0–10%.

2. *The cool referral.* They give you the details of a friend, acquaintance, or colleague, but call them to let them know who you are. Success rates here are as high as 30%.

3. *The personal introduction.* The customer not only calls the potential customer but also informs them about your company and your cooperation. They don't just pick up the phone; they arrange the appointment themselves. Success rates here amount to 50%.

4. *The face to face introduction.* Your client comes to the appointment with the potential client or invites him to your office. Success rates in that case are around 95–100%.

A.S., founder and CEO of Generation Y, now works almost exclusively by recommendation. Generation Y has been involved in digital transformation for 20 years. It has customers in 24 countries, including well-known names such as Starwood, a group of more than 1,150 hotels worldwide, Johns Hopkins University in Baltimore, the Volkswagen Group, Alumil, Toi Moi, Lapin stores, and many more.

He believes that Generation Y customers trust it precisely because it gives them measurable results before proceeding to invest, for its international experience, but also for the fact that everything runs smoothly within the company, creating products at the customer's discretion.

"We never say goodbye to a project. Cooperating with a customer is eternal as we never stop pursuing its goals, whether it's in marketing or sales or recording behavioral characteristics of its potential customers."

It didn't start out like that though.

At the age of 18, he asked his father to buy him a car. His father paid for his driving licence, but demanded he pay for the car himself. He decided to start designing websites. He found a partner—a software developer—and started to look for customers.

"So, I opened the Yellow Pages and counted the phone calls I made. One, two, three . . . hours later, one hundred. You can probably imagine how an 18-year-old who'd never worked before felt, and after a hundred phone calls had nothing to show for it but a slap in the face and zero interest from clients.

"At that moment, my girlfriend called and wanted to meet. Despite my despair, I managed to resist and continue the phone calls. The goal was still there, even though it wouldn't have taken much more to give up on it. As soon as I hung up the phone, my best friend called, asking me if I wanted to play basketball with the guys. With great difficulty, I rejected my friend's proposal and immediately picked up the phone to make my 101st call. A crane company. I started the pitch, which after a 100 phone calls I had almost perfected, and the answer was 'Yes. I'm interested.'

"You probably realize how strange this was for me because I was so used to rejections and was unprepared for a positive answer.

"He asked me to meet him there and then. So, I hung up the phone, jumped into my grandmother's blue Mitsubishi Lancer '72 and hit the road, trying unsuccessfully to pick up some speed.

"I was so dazed, I forgot to release the hand brake.

"The deal was done the same afternoon.

"When my father saw I'd completed my first project and after following the progress of my work, he introduced me to a friend of his, who wanted to do something similar.

"His friend was an insurer, who wanted to help us create a brand in the marketplace. That's when I realized how quickly word gets around. Not just with insurers but with salespeople in general.

"Strategically, I decided to focus on anyone who could spread the word. There was no way I was going to miss out on a customer recommendation.

"Nowadays, we work almost exclusively with recommendations. There are 230 people in the group today and I do not have a sales department. Ninety-five percent of our customers come from a recommendation and the other 5% are people who found us because of the work we do or heard about us at a talk."

Do not worry about failures, worry about the chances you miss when you don't even try.

Jack Canfield,
Author

Everyone Is Not Your Customer.

Not all customers are the same. Some order large volumes, some small, some need a lot of time for support, some are more self-sufficient, some are determined while others are hesitant, some are loyal while others buy from anyone anywhere.

You can't possibly group them all together. How do you decide on how to approach them? Do you have to approach them all?

A few years ago, *The Front Runner*, starring Hugh Jackman, hit the cinema screen. Gary Hart, by all accounts, was the most prominent candidate for the 1987 US presidency.

He was forced to drop out of the race when a relatively small newspaper, the *Miami Herald*, published an article about the most popular senator's illicit affair.

The following night, at the offices of the legendary Washington Post, a group of journalists discussed new ethics in journalism. The publisher of the newspaper at the time told a story.

"On New Year's Eve, after the death of John F. Kennedy, US President Lyndon Johnson sat down for a drink with White House reporters. At some point, he gathered us around him and said:

"'Gentlemen, you may see a lot of women walking in and out of my suites and local hotels. I want you to be as discreet as you were with John.'

"And so we were!

"'Those were different times, Ben,' said an old journalist.

"'I agree, but why? Who decides this?' asked the publisher.

"'The readers,' was the answer.

"In other words, the customers.

"'What if customers want to see the candidates naked? Will we do it?' was the next question.

"No one answered.

"'Everyone is not your customer,' is the answer."

Those who want to see the candidates naked will have to buy another newspaper.

Successful men keep moving. They make mistakes but they don't quit.

Conrad Hilton
Founder of the Hilton Hotels

In *This Is Marketing*, Seth Godin recounts the experience of an American stand-up comedian who picked up the microphone and performed his act perfectly. But no one laughed. He was so confident in his material that failure grounded him abruptly. He thought of giving up.

Until he found out that the audience was a group of Italians who did not speak English at all and they just wanted to watch the Comedy Club. Sometimes, you are simply addressing the wrong audience. It is now considered a mistake to address all people, all over the world. You need to reach out to a group of 5,000 specific people—the target group for a product, and expand in the second phase.

When you start to design your product, you should bear in mind that there will be some customers who will know what you're doing and see the usefulness of what you are willing to sell. However, there will be some customers who will not see its value and wouldn't buy it because it's not for them.

> ❝ Learn from the mistakes of others. You can't live long enough to make them all yourself.

Eleanor Roosevelt
Former First Lady of the United States

PayPal was founded in 1998. In 1999, it began operating as a platform for money transfers between users and companies.

It didn't go well at first. Users were not using the platform, so to persuade the public to give it a try, they offered them money. They started with $20 per user who opened an account and another $20 if they recommended someone.

Soon, the amount decreased to $10 and then $5. They had already spent $65 million when they decided to stop to save the company from going bankrupt.

Then, they decided to approach eBay users. They optimized the platform for eBay, which was just starting up at the time, despite having doubts about their choice.

"What's this market all about? They buy and sell garbage," they said. Despite their doubts, the experiment proved to be successful. Within a short time, they acquired 25–30% of eBay customers and as this grew, so did PayPal's customer base. So, PayPal was a natural follow-on from eBay. They had created a brand and a customer base, so people began to look at them differently.

In 2002, PayPal was sold to eBay for $1.5 billion.

So, when you design a product, it should address the needs of the customer and have its own persona.

But, what is a persona?

A persona is a character assumed by an author in a written work, or a personality that a person projects in public. Here, the goal is to create a reliable and realistic representation of the market you are targeting.

To create a persona, you start by collecting data, creating a working hypothesis, and end with a detailed description of the person. This means that you have to determine the gender, age, income, level of education and work experience. You can also add a name or a photo.

Also, what other characteristics do they have?

Where do they live? Are they married? Do they have children?

Is that enough? No!

There should also be psychological variables, such as what motivates them, what they fear most, what are their values, what are their goals, what disappoints them, where they go on holiday and everything else that makes up a very specific personality.

To continue:

What products do they buy nowadays?

What features are they looking for in these products?

Why these products and not others?

How do they select them?

How much money are they willing to spend on them?

Where do they get their information from? Which websites, newsletters, applications do they use to stay informed?

Do they watch TV? Which channels?

Do they listen to the radio? Which stations?
Which type of events do they participate in?

At Entranet, we created Frank Martin.

Frank Martin is German, 45 years old, married with two children—a 13-year-old girl and a boy of 10. He is upper-middle class. His mother is no longer alive, and his father lives alone in a village, about 200 kilometres away.

Frank is a business executive and travels a lot. He likes innovation and deals with technology on a daily basis. He is worried about his father's health but also about his family because he is often away from home.

Frank's father is called Eric. He is middle-class, lives alone, knows nothing about technology and prefers to shop locally. He doesn't see his children very often and has some issues with his health, which he keeps a close eye on. Being burgled, isolation and being a burden to his children are what he fears most. Death is ranked below all of these.

Entranet's housemate smart home package is aimed at anyone who is building, renovating, or buying a home. We have to think in terms of:

'What would the user want in this case?'

In Frank's case, it's pretty obvious. Frank has also helped us with dealings with our investors. His persona clarifies the picture for them. They understand our market.

Everyone is not your customer.

Seth Godin
Marketing Expert

There are many examples of products that started off to meet a certain need or to target a certain clientele, but the customer had a different point of view.

Xerox began making photocopiers for professionals. The market research they did along the way concluded that professionals did not need this type of machine. But businesses, universities, schools, and many individuals did.

The German chemist who discovered the first local anaesthetic novocaine in 1905 tried to pass it on to doctors who had given their patients general anesthesia until then. None of the surgeons were willing to use it. Until a dentist tried it and the product was discovered on the market.

The same thing happened with the computer. Remington Rand made Univac, the first computer for scientific work. It was an amazing machine they never thought to promote to individuals. IBM, on the other hand, also created a computer for research purposes, but never refused to sell it to anyone who wanted to buy it, whether it was a business or an individual. 10 years later, Remington Rand still had the best machine, but IBM had won over the computer market. Consequently, the message from the marketplace is once again clear.

Companies that insist on the original design and do not correctly understand the customers they are targeting, are certain to pay for it in the process.

Always do your best. Whatever you plant now, you will harvest later.

Og Mandino,
Author

Do Not Chase the Giants

In 2014, talk2lift hit the market. We started to get some exploratory queries as well as some small orders. Elevator companies were wary of our product and needed more time.

Then we decided to approach the world-leading Otis Elevator Company. With offices around the world and a turnover of $15.8 billion in 2014, it seemed the ideal client.

I remember talking with my associates and saying that if we did a deal with a client like that, we wouldn't need any others.

Today, we can't believe how naive we were.

To go back to the story, sometime later, the Otis European Research and Development Center opened the door to us in Gien, France. We arrived on a Thursday night and stayed at a local hotel before our 9am appointment at the company's offices on the Friday morning.

The Otis employees, who were very welcoming, took us to the meeting room. After the presentation, we agreed to send a demo in French, with wiring diagrams and a user manual.

Two weeks later, they'd received them. And then, we waited. Another two weeks passed without news. We'd received no replies to the emails we'd sent.

A month later, I got hold of an engineer we had met at the presentation on the phone. He politely explained to us that they had not yet opened the box and hoped to do so at some point in the second half of the year because their schedule was tight.

Then, I decided to try and contact the Otis' parent company in Connecticut, USA. I informed them I'd be in New York the following month and would be willing to make the three-and-a-half-hour journey to their offices and demonstrate talk2lift.

After several attempts, I was accepted and given a specific date and time for the meeting. It was a Wednesday morning, and it was raining. I arrived at the boardroom a few minutes early after driving for nearly four hours in very difficult conditions.

The Otis executives' reaction was very positive. They considered talk2lift an interesting alternative to the system for the visually impaired designed and implemented by their German colleagues a few years earlier. So, they asked us to present our technology to their partners at the factory in Germany.

Three months later, and with the French researchers having yet to open the box, a meeting was held at the Otis electronics factory outside Berlin.

Here, I must add that it was the beginning of 2014, and Greece's reputation in Europe, especially in Germany, was at a historic low. The presentation went smoothly, and the engineers placed an order for two units to carry out the necessary tests.

They were the last $16 billion the giant ever bought.

The message was clear.

There are neither large nor small customers, to begin with. You realize this along the way because you can always take on a big job from a small client, and on the other hand, you can get tangled up for years chasing the 'giant' with no results.

This is exactly what the Domissima Export Manager experienced, too.

In 2012, a large shopping center was being built in Bulgaria. With some careful handling, the sale closed immediately. The local partner of Domissima received an immediate deposit of €10,000 to start the project.

On the way back, a potential customer called him asking for information. The Export Manager exchanged information and details for 45 minutes. At the end, the customer said,

"I'll need your help with something. For the job I want to do, your small bag is not big enough and the large one is bigger than I need. Could your partner give me half a bag?"

'We talked for 45 minutes about half a bag?
What was that all about?' he thought to himself.

He replied that this was impossible, but he'd see if the dealer could give him a better price. And that's what happened. He spoke to a store manager immediately and the client's request was satisfied.

Eight months later, his phone rang. It was a familiar voice.

It was the same man. This guy mentioned the name of a salesman who had shown great interest, to a friend who was building a hotel. In the end, Domissima closed a huge deal because one salesman would spend 45 minutes on someone who needed half a bag of their product.

 Don't find customers for your products, find products for your customers.

Seth Godin
Marketing Expert

Returning to Connecticut, let's go back half a century. In 1964 at Yale University, Fred Smith, an economics student, submitted his assignment on Overnight Shipping, in other words, the method of transporting goods known today as a courier service. His tutor didn't appreciate the idea and gave the student a C minus. He graduated in 1966 and joined the Marines. He returned in 1969 and decided to put forward his idea. And FedEx, the first courier company in the world was born.

Fred had noticed a malfunction when customers of different banks exchanged checks. Usually, when someone gave a New York bank check to someone who deposited it at a bank in California, the process was time-consuming and risky. It was because the New York bank had to send the check to the state central bank and the central bank had to send the check to the central bank of the California, which took around 10 days. If the check bounced, the beneficiary was in trouble. The original idea was to create a company to deliver the checks to their final destination overnight.

The first level of the agreement was reached.

He decided to name the company Federal Express, given that its client would be the US Central Bank, the Federal Reserve.

Fred Smith bought two Falcon jets using his own money and investor funds. Everything was progressing well until the day the central bank decided to withdraw from the deal.

This could have been the end of the company. A huge amount of money had been invested in a company that had only one client. When this customer ceased to exist, this would very easily lead to the bankruptcy of the company. And this usually happens to companies that place all their hopes and depend on one customer for their entire turnover. The story could have ended here, at least for this book. But since the marketplace is magical and full of incredible stories, I will carry on.

In this particular case, the entrepreneur did not give up. He presented the idea to investors and raised $91 million. He bought another 12 Falcons, and his fleet was now able to transport goods to 25 states.

In 1973, the OPEC countries decided to impose an oil embargo on America. Fuel prices, which accounted for FedEx's main operating costs, doubled with the company unable to raise fares.

In July of that year, FedEx had $5,000 in its reserves. The fuel bill for the week was $24,000.

Then, in a spur of the moment decision, Fred Smith took the money from the reserves, went to Las Vegas, and gambled it all at the casino on a game of Blackjack. He won $27,000 and stayed afloat for one more week.

The following week, the founder of FedEx found new investors and is currently the top courier business in the world.

 The customer's perception is your reality.

Kate Zabriskie,
Author

Some think that the largest and highest consuming markets in the world are ideal for them and their products. And they may be right. There are companies whose products will only succeed on the other side of the Atlantic. So, the decision is more or less predetermined.

However, I would suggest you to bear a few things in mind beforehand and incorporate them into your business plan. Obviously, if it's necessary to appeal to the American market, you should calculate that every appointment will cost much more, especially if you are located in Europe or Asia. It could cost you as much as it would take to keep your company afloat for another month. The month you need to launch your product.

Then you need to promote your product and for that you'll need a huge amount of money. If you don't have it, your product will likely never see the light of day.

So, if you don't have the money to make the necessary moves, don't start out in countries where the process is very expensive.

 It takes months to find a customer . . . seconds to lose one.

Vince Lombardi,
Player and Coach

Summer 2015. Entranet had just presented its second product at the Smart Home World Summit in London. It was the housemate, the first voice enabled smart home control device in the world.

After the exhibition we returned to Greece. The next day a referendum was announced. And the day after, capital controls were inforced. Total collapse . . .

For the first time in my career, I laid down on the floor of my office and looked at the ceiling. We were losing talk2lift customers because we couldn't import circuit boards, and therefore export products. I couldn't travel abroad because we were only allowed to withdraw €60 a day and were unable to use our credit cards outside Greece. I was trapped by whatever change would come next.

Just as I was thinking I should probably wait for the storm to pass and see what remained standing, I received an email. The Vice-Chairman of one of the largest companies in the world, whom I met on a trip to America, informed me that he would be in Thessaloniki for a day during his holidays and would like to see me. We talked for two hours and decided to meet again at the company's headquarters in New Jersey the following month. We were all excited at Entranet. Maybe this stroke of luck could help us with something that had been violently interrupted.

The following month, we visited their offices. The presentation of our technology to the leaders of the $45 billion turnover colossus went extremely well.

We met again the same week to discuss how to proceed. When we returned to Greece, a non-disclosure agreement was reached, and an engagement contract was signed.

It was our first contract with the 'Giant'.

In November 2015, we sent a device carrying the technology we had developed. And just like with Otis the year before, we waited . . . and waited . . .

By the end of January 2016, we finally received an email summing up the conclusion of the global company's R&D team.

"[. . .] We believe that Entranet's technology could add value to 'Giant' products."

Finally! The road seemed to be opening.

Once more, we waited . . .

Two months later, it was announced that the company would proceed with neither a buyout offer nor a collaboration offer for reasons that could not be revealed. We found out along the way that they had acquired another start-up with similar technology for a huge amount two years ago. The acquisition of a new company with a similar product would create internal problems for their associates who had approved the previous expensive deal. And no one wants problems.

No one.

Especially the giant companies.

" How you sell matters. But how your customers feel when they engage with you matters more.

Tiffany Bova,
Author

Communicate, Feel, Connect!

In the United Kingdom elections of 1874, the working class led by William Gladstone was overwhelmingly defeated by the conservatives of Benjamin Disraeli.

The animosity between the two leaders was huge. This was not a simple confrontation. The conflict had begun many years earlier. They were both leaders of their parties from 1868 but were dominant figures long before that and people of great intelligence.

They had very different social backgrounds. Gladstone was a member of the wealthy upper-middle-class, studied at Eton and Christ Church College, Oxford.

Disraeli's parents were of Italian descent. His father was a distinguished, educated man and the young Disraeli was raised an Anglican.

Some years after the departure of both from the central political scene, the former prime ministers met at a baroness' dinner. After the two men had departed, the baroness left the reception area to answer journalists' questions.

The first journalist's question was:

"How did you feel talking to Mr Gladstone?"

and the answer was,

"When I spoke to Mr Gladstone, I felt he was the most interesting man in the world."

Immediately after, another journalist asked the obvious question:

"How did you feel talking to Mr Disraeli?"

"When I spoke to Mr Disraeli, I felt that I was the most interesting person in the world."

What did Mr Disraeli know that Mr Gladstone didn't? He used his ears and his mouth proportionately. He knew to listen with his ears, eyes, head, and heart. That's how you win over people, voters, customers, and friends!

Theodore Levitt, a Harvard professor said, "People don't want a quarter-inch drill. They want a quarter-inch hole. The drill is a means to an end."

The reasoning, however, continues. Nobody really wants a hole in the wall. They want to hang something. A painting, a photograph, a shelf. If we take it even further, they don't even want the painting or the photo. They want the feeling they get after hanging the photo.

It may be their daughter's first birthday, which brings back beautiful memories. Maybe they want the feeling they get when their wife says, "Well done!" At the end of the day, they buy two things: first, memories and nice feelings, and second, the satisfaction that they did it themselves, which again has to do with the emotions. Other times, people want to feel safe and calm, to relax in a tidy living room at the end of a working day.

At the end of the day, what they're buying is security, peace of mind and good feelings, even if they started out to buy a simple drill.

The product you sell must cover what the buyer wants to feel. If you just add more functions or think only about how to sell it and forget how the buyer will feel, you're making a serious mistake.

 Pretend that every single person you meet has a sign around his or her neck that says, 'make me feel important.' Not only will you succeed in sales, you will succeed in life.

Mary Kay Ash
Founder of Mary Kay Cosmetics

I had a great conversation with N.D., award-winning communications consultant, and Director of the Western

Balkans Department of the International Faculty of the University of Sheffield, based in Belgrade.

"The brain has a ram, a functionality memory. When you download too much onto your computer, it crashes. The same goes for the brain. If there are too many stimulants or if something unexpected happens and it needs to act, it will likely crash.

"So, what does it do? The brain is constantly trying to find a strategy to minimise 'pain' and maximize 'gain'. It continuously revises strategies every second of the day. Energy is precious, you see! The brain accounts for 2% of the body and consumes 20% of its energy. So, most of the things the brain does aim to conserve energy. That is its single purpose.

"On the other hand, it gets terribly bored! Let me tell you something amazing. There's another feature called 'entanglement'.

"Here we can see how many neurons the brain invests in something. That is, how important it considers it to be. If something is very important, it will invest more neurons from various points. If it is not important, it will save its energy. But where feelings are concerned, everything changes. A larger part of the brain's attention gets involved to capture the message you want to relate.

"On the other hand, even this has changed. The emotional threshold has risen. The younger generation is indifferent to things that used to make us cry or sad. To get the attention of people nowadays,

you have to climb five emotional steps and hit them
hard on the head! Only then you can sell!"

In their book *Switch*, authors Chip and Dan Heath state that
we have two selves. The logical self that makes the plans, and
the emotional self that acts. These two selves interact like a
75kg rider on a five-ton elephant. When the rider thinks they
should move northwards, but the elephant has decided not to
move, arguments will not help in the least.

Therefore, the most successful commercials in recent
years have been those that tell stories inspired by family,
friendship, and human relationships to the sounds of
emotionally charged music.

 Companies should be selling ideas more than benefits.
Sell ideas, not stuff.

Aaron Ross,
CEO of Predictable Revenue Inc

When billionaire businessman Mark Cuban took over the
Dallas Mavericks, the only distinction the team had received in
the last decade was the award for the NBA's worst corporate
management. The new management took on the bold task
of filling the empty seats in the stadium. All the salespeople
gathered in one big open-plan office and looked at the lists
of people that had bought anything in the past, from ordinary
tickets to season tickets. Mark Cuban made the first phone
calls from the middle of the room because,

"If they didn't see me doing it, how could they be

persuaded to do the same?"

So, he picked up the phone and said:

"Hello! This is Mark Cuban, the new owner of the Dallas Mavericks. Knowing you've bought tickets in the past, I'd just like to say we'd be delighted to see you at the stadium again."

That's where complaints about the team image, lack of organization and mismanagement began. There was no point in listing facts and information.

"We decided we'd address our fans' feelings."

"Do you know that going to the stadium is cheaper than going to McDonald's? Do you know that we now have tickets costing less than a visit to the cinema? With this money, you and your family can experience something unique that you won't find anywhere else," he continued.

The protests continued until he asked them if they remembered when their parents took them to the stadium for the first time.

Their voices softened and there was a slight pause, which signaled nostalgia.

"Do you remember how you felt?"

A pause followed by a happy 'yes! 'at the other end of the line.

"Do you feel the same when you go to McDonald's? Probably not . . .

"Well, we can't promise we'll go back to winning right away but we can guarantee a unique experience. We guarantee that nowhere else will make you feel like you do when you look at the smiles on your children's faces. And for such an experience, we have tickets that start at $8.'

"Sale closed. People returned to the stands. The team made revenue and won the NBA championship in the process. Because, as Maya Angelou, writer, and poet, used to say,

"'I have learned that people will forget what you said, people will forget what you did but they will never forget how you made them feel.'"

And that is the key.

That's why in costly Coca Cola ads, you don't hear anyone describe the taste. Nor the properties of the caffeine contained in the bottle. You only see happy smiling faces, friends, special family moments and warmth and enjoyment instead. The same goes for Nike advertisements. Have you ever heard Nike mention new air soles, dynamic lines, or the durability of their shoes? Of course not!

An unforgettable scene from the movie *What Women Want* is where advertiser Nick Marshall (Mel Gibson) presented the Nike women's line campaign.

I have to remind you that after an accident in his bathroom, Nick can hear what women are thinking. He gradually begins to understand how they feel, and the presentation goes like this:

"You don't stand in front of the mirror before you go out running thinking what the road will think of your outfit. You don't have to laugh at the road's jokes to run. It won't be easier to run if you dress provocatively. The road won't notice if you're wearing lipstick and doesn't care how old you are. You won't feel bad because you earn more money than it.

"And you can see it whenever you want to. It won't complain that it's been a week, a day or even a couple of hours since you last met. The only thing the road cares about is that you visit it once in a while. Nike. No games. Just sports!"

"Where do we sign?" said the three ladies on the panel. Why? Because feelings are the only things that count.

I spoke to D.T., personal and professional development consultant and author of the book *Escape from the Cave*.

"The magic word is feeling," he said.

"Can you stir people's emotions? That's where they'll follow you. They'll believe in what you believe in. Can I convince you that by buying my product or service, you're participating in something bigger than a simple act of buying and selling?

"This is the key.

"Because if what I'm selling only makes sense as far as my wallet and personal ambitions are concerned, it'll show. The other person will have no reason to take part in it. You may win that customer over some other time but only if they are desperate for what you are selling. And if that's the case, you can be sure that as soon as they find something similar at a better price, they'll drop you without a second thought.

"The same goes for colleagues and employees. If the person you work with for eight to 10 hours every day doesn't believe there's a greater meaning to what they're doing, they'll leave at the first chance. With the first better financial offer they get. You can't pretend. It has to be true. It has to be genuine.

"Not just for customers, but for colleagues, employees and whoever else you want to follow what you stand for.

"A typical story is that of the Toms. Blake Mycoskie's 'one for one concept'.

"This man started a company to make shoes for a better tomorrow, which he wanted to call Tomorrow's Shoes.

"As this could not be printed on the side of the shoes, he shortened it to 'Toms'.

"How did it all start? In 2006, Blake was 29 years old and had already founded his fourth start-up. He'd set up a laundry on a university campus, receiving and delivering clothes to students, an advertising company, an online reality channel, and a 'green' online driving school with virtual hybrid cars.

"Blake had promised himself to go to Argentina. There, he tried to lose himself in the culture of the people, learning the tango, playing their national sport of polo, and drinking local wine. He also started wearing the local shoe, the alpargata, which was an easy-to-make, soft shoe that locals wore everywhere.

"A few days before returning to America, he

met an American woman in a cafe. She told him that many children—even in developed countries—had no shoes and this had a direct impact on their daily lives. In certain areas, these children could not go to school or carry water home. At the same time, it was the source of numerous diseases.

"His first thought was to help these children by asking friends and relatives for donations. He knew this would have limited results and then realized what needed to be done. He was a start-up founder, after all.

"So, he set up Toms, where for every pair of shoes the company sold, another went to a child in need.

"To date, more than 2,000,000 new pairs of shoes have been given to children in 50 countries such as The Philippines, Cambodia, Lesotho, South Africa, Peru, and Honduras.

"Blake carries on relentlessly. He recently wrote the book *Start Something That Matters*, and for every book sold, Toms provides books to needy children. Toms is the definition of a company that created a fan club instead of a clientele. Can you do that? Of course you can! As long as you display and stir emotion."

PART 3

The heart is closer to the pocket than the brain is. People buy emotionally and then justify logically.

Michael R. Virardi,
Speaker and Writer

So, at the End of the Day, What Does the Customer Want?

After 24 rules, 24 interviews, sales and marketing training programs, countless books and videos, I have come to one conclusion: Some things are so heavily imprinted on our minds that instinct becomes invincible. I was under the impression we'd made significant steps forward since hunter-gatherer times. To a large extent, I was wrong!

Maybe what the customer actually wants is no surprise.

Contemporary consumer behavior is indeed surprising, however, and the start-up

LEFTERIS PAPAGEORGIOU

founder is required to understand needs that often seem absurd.

But are they really absurd?

I discussed this with Konstantinos Petsanis, a behavioral neurologist and consultant at the World Health Organization, and I was unsurprised by many of his answers. I return to the questions I asked at the beginning of the book.

LP: **How do you explain the fact that it took Facebook took two and a half years to reach 50 million customers, WhatsApp 15 years, and yet Angry Birds, just 15 days? Why did people pay for a game where slingshots launch birds at smiling pigs?**

KP: To get where we are today, where the sun is no longer a god but used to power photovoltaic panels, we went through various phases. From ignorance to a source of energy. When social networks like Facebook appeared on the scene, we didn't really know what they were or how to use them. It was like coming out of the cave, seeing something unknown and cautiously approaching it. When Facebook whetted man's appetite for information, curiosity piqued. It filled the human need for gossip and protected exposure at the same time, like a person who swears inside his car but keeps a safe distance when he gets out of it. And we took it on board. And the road was opened up by WhatsApp. Compared to Skype, Facebook, and other communication applications, it was simple. And that was it! To understand the success of Angry Birds, we need to understand that modern man has an inherent need to 'destroy'. The ability to break, dissolve or destroy creates a sense of relief. It's a primitive need. And people hit pigs. A pig means dirt, muck. By hitting them, you hit what's bad and dirty. In other words, by hitting a pig, an animal, a primitive reaction is released.

LP: **Why does a person spend €100,000 on a four-wheeler when they never leave the city center?**

KP: There are two reasons for this. The first is fashion. How was this fashion created? Nowadays, all women wear black sunglasses. Why? Humans have a primitive tendency to homogenise in groups. Because if a person stands out, it causes a lot of stress. They don't have to back it up.

But if they look the same as everyone else in the group, they will never need to back it up. It justifies itself and wastes less energy. In the caveman days, if you came out into the light and saw 50 people turning right and one person turning left, and you followed the person who turned left, you were attacked by a bear and the bear would eat you. Your DNA would not survive. If you followed the 50 people turning right, your life would be in much less danger. And your DNA would survive. Let's talk about the second reason. I want to look big. This philosophy has been around for a long time, starting with kings and priests. They all wore crowns.

Noblemen and the rich wore tall hats. African tribal leaders wore tall headgear. To look taller, bigger. A man's personality is automatically identified by his car. These are difficult times for men. His prehistoric need to demonstrate his manhood continues to exist without him having the means to do so. He wants to attract, be seen and stand out from other males. We're going back to those times because society is weaker.

LP: **Why does a customer spend €5,000 on the latest sound system for their car when they don't even have a radio at home? Even for a small car.**

KP: But it's the car that people see. It's the car by which they'll be judged. They won't be judged by their house. Their house is not on display. The woman they want to attract won't come to their house. At least not at first. But she'll get into their car.

So nowadays, the car is bait. The male hunter's car is his weapon. It's where he'll be seen so that's where he'll invest. He may not have a radio at home, but by the time the house comes into play, the game's over and the car has achieved its goal.

LP: **Why does an item that's been lingering on the shelf for ages sell out as soon as you announce it'll only be available for two more days?**

KP: As long as it's there, you take it for granted. You see it in the window, and you think it'll be there next week, next month. You'll buy it when you have the money. But if it's only available for two more days, things change. It makes you feel insecure.

LP: Why does wine taste better if it's served from a heavier bottle?

KP: If you put it in a plastic bottle, it tastes even worse. Here, we must look at the information the brain receives and the conclusions it draws. Don't forget, we grew up with glass milk bottles which then became plastic. Everyone knew this was done to make it cheaper. The heavier something is, the more it is worth. When someone gives you a wedding invitation, what are they doing? They could send you an email with the details. They could give you a photocopy with the same information. Yet they don't. They usually deliver it by hand instead of posting it. Heavy, expensive, well-designed invitations. The brain gets the message that this is important. With precious gems, the heavier they are, the more expensive they are. So, all those years of brainwashing make you think a heavier bottle serves better wine.

LP: Why do people think their cars perform better when they're clean?

KP: My house is extremely functional when it is tidy. When my clothes are scattered about, it's unacceptable; I live in a mess. A clean car, relatively speaking, is important. Its silhouette and its value stand out. The exact opposite happens when it's dirty. It gives me the impression it's not transporting me properly. All of this is based on the brain's ability to create contrast. The brain works by contrasting. The bigger the contrast in shape, the clearer an object becomes and is easier to take in. If the outline is difficult to distinguish, it's more confusing. The more indistinguishable the shape is, the less we appreciate it. A scratched iPhone puts you off its function. It may be problem-free, but you think it needs replacing. This is how we function, we are prone to illusion, and consider a non-functional object with clear lines better than a neglected product of higher value. Clearly, we think with our eyes.

LP: **Why do airline passengers feel safer if there are no advertisements on the outside of the plane?**

KP: Airline customers want the plane to look clean. If it is, they feel safe. They consider it to be neat and well-maintained. They do not want advertisements on the body of the aircraft because the plane is not a billboard. It must be treated with due reverence and respect because it carries human souls. If you treat the plane as a billboard, you are undermining your customers' confidence. On the other hand, white planes are difficult to keep clean. But this is how they show passengers that the aircraft is well maintained.

LP: **Why has Uber been so successful, even in countries where taxi services are of the highest standard?**

KP: Uber revolutionized paid transport, not because it came up with high-flying innovation, but mainly because it provided a method via your mobile phone to see where your taxi will pick you up and how long it will take to get to you.

Surveys have shown that people feel particularly uncomfortable in uncertain situations. For the same reason, informing London underground passengers when the next train would arrive was more acceptable than attempting to reduce the waiting time between routes. Why?

Because the passenger feels better if they have to wait eight minutes and know about it than wait four minutes without knowing when the next train will arrive!

LP: **Why do you think something's 15% cheaper when you make a contactless payment?**

KP: This is typical of our generation. I'm not at all sure it will apply to future generations. Don't forget, we were taught that buying something meant taking a precious piece of paper out of your pocket and giving it away. We give something material, and we get something material. Your pocket feels lighter. You clearly feel the energy. Before that, we would have handed over 20 eggs and got a sheep in return. It was an exchange. You felt it. After that, money was used. It took time for people to get used to the idea that they got a chicken in exchange for pieces of paper. Now you wave a card over a machine to pay, and you don't feel the exchange. The same card goes back into your pocket. The material remains the same, so it must be cheaper.

LP: **Why do they try to make neutral-flavored drugs taste worse?**

KP: Because if the taste is not bad, it is not medication. Can you imagine if drugs were sweet-tasting? That would be a different problem. The user must feel that the drug they are taking will face evil. It's a dirty, tough warrior. If it's sweet, they don't believe it will do the job. On the other hand, if I give you a bitter-tasting sweet and tell you it's a pill, you'll be fine in half an hour.

LP: **Why do painkillers work best if they come in a red box and even better if the company that produces them is well-known?**

KP: Here we come to the philosophy on which the placebo effect was built. Nature's colors give us the sense that something is natural. If a medication is white or green, you can take it without fear. But at the same time, you believe that even if you do not take this medication, it makes no difference! When clinical trials for the placebo were carried out, users seemed to be convinced that if they took the green pill, nothing would happen. If they took the blue pill, they had taken poison. It was very strong medication. You admit the white pill is an antibiotic but to get the job done, you have to take the blue one. The same phenomenon applies to the red box. What color is inflammation? Inflammation is red. You can't imagine it in any other way. Phlegm, fire, red. It's a connotation that won't allow you to see it any other way. So, the box must be a firefighter! What color is the fire department? Red. But why? It discharges water, shouldn't it be blue? An eye for an eye. I throw something red on the fire. Blue does not fit here because the poison talked about earlier, will not work on flames. In this case, I must fight the fire with something similar.

LP: **Why do people buy champagne for cats?**

KP: That is obvious. Human loneliness is a huge problem in today's society. And so are human relationships. Many people have resorted to solving these problems with animals. They are trying to overcome their problematic relationship with people. Everything unfolds from that. Cat sweaters, cat perfumes, cat groomers, cat baskets, cat lounge seats on planes and . . . yes, champagne for cats! Why?

Because the cat is my companion. It makes me feel complete. Why not treat my cat like I would treat a friend?

It's hyperbolic, if not paranoic to substitute human contact with a pet.

LP: **Why do people buy lights that fit into the toilet basin?**

KP: A lot of people are very worried about their health. There are people who cough into their hands to see if they spat any blood. They blow their nose and check the handkerchief. They look in the mirror, not to see how beautiful they are, but to look for signs that could be symptoms of disease. They always look at their urine and feces because they know that by doing so, they'll see if anything is wrong. If I check my feces, I think everything is fine. There is no cause for concern. So, there will always be a buyer for the light in the toilet basin.

LP: Should start-up founders become psychologists after all?

KP: Start-up founders have to build a team. And it's a good idea to have someone in their team who understands what the customer wants.

While writing this book, I was a bit insecure. You google the term sales and you get seven billion results. What could I write that was worth your time? However, after gathering material and recording my thoughts and experiences, I came up with a very specific answer to the question: *What does the customer want?*

In my humble opinion, dear start-up founder, the customer wants to feel safe. They want the person they are dealing with not to take advantage of them or expose them.

They want someone who will:
- offer them the best deal;
- gain their trust;
- respect their time, understand their problem and offer a solution to that problem;
- know their product and what the competition offers;
- act as a consultant, not a salesman;
- show genuine interest;
- ask and listen to the answer;
- have a story worth participating in;

- be prepared;
- handle the negotiation properly; and
- close it when all concerned have benefited.

In the end, we are all the same. The people you are dealing with have families, difficult schedules, problems, and financial issues to solve. They have a job to do, just like you. Respect it and demand the same respect from them. Try to understand how you would feel and what you would like. You both want the same thing: an easy, quick, beneficial agreement with no problems and second thoughts.

On the other hand, the customer wants to solve problems in the easiest possible way—without having to deal with them. He wants someone to take the weight off his shoulders, without feeling he is being used. The package must contain a very good deal, a problem solved, and the acquisition of much more than the money they spent.

At the end of the day, you are the customer.

And so am I.

And for sure, we both want all of the above.

Final Thoughts

When I was writing my first book, the president of Quest Technologies, Theodore Fessas, said,

"Having a start-up is like driving a car at high speed on a winding, mountain road with poor visibility. You can't take your eyes off the road because you'll drive off a cliff. You have no way of knowing if, after the next bend, the road will open up and become a highway. Maybe it will never open up."

I must add that the only thing you do know is how much petrol you have in your tank. You have to get as far as possible with that amount of fuel and hope to see the highway open before you. The only way to do this is to sell your product to continue to fuel the vehicle for as long as it takes. So, this is the time for results. The design was successful, and you have to move on!

I saved a personal story for the ending.

In 1991, I got into the Department of Civil Engineering at the Aristotle University in Thessaloniki. After studying for two years, the only thing I cared about was the radio station I was working at. I was the producer of a successful show and the head of advertising and public relations for the station. I was having a great time and making a living at the same time. However, the pressure from my father at home was constantly increasing. He preached on and on.

"When will you start at an engineering firm to learn the job? Who will hire you when you don't even know the color of concrete?"

In 1998, shortly before I finished my military service, I sent out a CV to a huge insulating materials manufacturer. To everyone's surprise, they selected me out of 50 applicants. Why? Because they needed an engineer to make presentations to other engineers all over Europe, and I was the only one who was familiar with a microphone. Needless to say, my father never said anything about my career again.

Along the way, I set up 17 ventures in five countries, sold eight of them, and had one that was a disaster. A disaster that could have ruined everything I'd built in my first 12 years of work.

In 2009, I came across some statistics that made me realize that the construction sector would suffer greatly for the next 10 to 15 years. It was then that I founded Entranet.

I still remember what surprised me—I felt ready enough to launch my first start-up. On the other hand, if you trust the statistics, you should never create a start-up since so many of them are set up every year and 95% close down, the majority of them within the first year. Friends that had failed by taking the same path before were left with a bitter sweet memory. 'I tried,' 'I gave it my all.' Why do we do it, then?

Why do we try to create a team to fight against the odds that clearly show you're walking off the edge of a cliff?

If someone offered you a huge amount of money to parachute from a plane, knowing that 9 times out of 10, the parachute will not open, would you do it? Certainly not. So why?

Here, I will borrow an answer from Yoshiro Nakamatsu. Currently in his 90s, he has filed 3,752 patents, (three times as many as Thomas Edison) for various inventions; from useless objects, such as shoes that take you to your destination in leaps, a chair with a built-in hood for better thinking, to two useful, complex machines for industry. The super old man is still going. Five years ago, doctors diagnosed him with a rare form of cancer, giving him 12 months to live. He decided to 'invent' a way out. So, he designed a system that consisted of a special diet, a radiation machine and exercise at the bottom of a swimming pool, forcing himself to extremes, rising for air a few seconds before drowning. Madness? Maybe.

However, he is still here.

Dr Nakamatsu considers himself young. He says he will continue to invent things until he dies. Because he discovered that making other people happy is what makes him happy. And he does it by solving problems with his inventions—exactly what start-ups do. The legendary Steve Jobs used to say that you cannot connect the dots from beginning to end.

Only when you look back, you can see where each of those steps took you.

Looking back, I realize it was the radio that gave me my first job as an engineer; a job that required me to present insulating materials to engineers and clients all over Europe. So when the time came, I was ready to present my own start-up to investors and clients all around the world for Entranet!

You never know where the next step will take you.

I am absolutely certain, however, about one thing. Each step is part of a magical journey. To experience it, you have to 'walk the mile.' Live the process of creation, the process of design and execution! And then sell it.

This will create added value and jobs.

And you'll be writing a story worth sharing!

Acknowledgment

To write this book, I received help from many people and owe them a big thank you. I want to thank Christina Lykopoulou for the design and editing of my second book.

I also have to thank my good friends Christos Ritzoulis and Mimis Alichanidis for their constructive criticism and advice.

I am most grateful to my friends and associates Prodromos Nikolaidis and Konstantinos Zavos for the help and support they have offered in recent years with the business development of Entranet, or in short, because they were always there for me.

I also want to thank the people who shared their stories with me. The stories that were recalled in the previous pages. I value these stories more than anything.

In closing, I apologize to my wife, Dimitra, and my children, Eliza and Apostolos, for the summer they spent practically alone, so I could write the book you have just read.

About the Author

Lefteris Papageorgiou is the CEO of Entranet, running the entire spectrum of the company's (Florida, London, and Thessaloniki) day-to-day operations.

He has more than 25 years of experience in construction, technology, and sustainable energy projects. He has been a successful entrepreneur with 17 ventures in five countries.

Many of the companies he founded were acquired by European investors.

He studied at the Aristotle University of Thessaloniki, where he received his Master's of Science in civil engineering.

He is a public speaker, having delivered talks and seminars at various events around the world.

Also, Lefteris is the author of the bestseller, *Start-ups. An Idea to the Global Market*, which was published in December 2018.

References

BOOKS AND VIDEOS

1. Virardi, Michael R. 2010. *Positive Impact: 26 Simple Ways to Boost Your Business and Your Life*. BookBaby.
2. Kampouraki, Dimitri. *A Drop of History*. Patakis Publications.
3. Kampouraki, Dimitri. *A Drop of Histoyr: Part Two*. Patakis Publications.
4. Anchor, Shawn. 2011. *The Happiness Advantage*. United Kingdom: Virgin Books.
5. Girard, Joe. 2006. *How to Sell Anything to Anybody*. Simon & Schuster.
6. Heath, Chip and Dan Heath. 2011. *Switch: How to Change Things When Change Is Hard*. United Kingdom: Random House Business Books.

7. Goldstein, Noah J., Steve J. Martin, and Robert B. Cialdini. 2013. *YES! 50 Secrets from the Science of Persuasion.* Profile Books Ltd.

8. Ziglar, Zig. 1985. *Zig Ziglar's Secrets Of Closing The Sale: For Anyone Who Must Get Others to Say Yes!* USA: Berkley.

9. Vaynerchuk, Gary. 2018, *Crushing it! How Great Entrepreneurs Build their Business and Influence and How You Can, Too.* USA: Harper Business.

10. Cram, Tony. 2001. *Customers that Count: How to Build Living Relationships with Your Most Valuable Customers.* Financial Times/Prentice Hall.

11. Holmes, Chet. 2008. *The Ultimate Sales Machine.* Penguin Portfolio.

12. Fleming, Noah and Shawn Veltman. 2017. *Dealing with Difficult Customers: How to Turn Demanding, Dissatisfied, and Disagreeable Clients into Your Best.* USA: New Page Books.

13. Content Marketing Institute. 2015. " The Story of Content: Rise of the New Marketing." *YouTube.* Video, 43:41. September 9.
    https://www.youtube.com/watch?v=dBnpr3pkFlk

14. Today I Found Out. 2019. "The Legendary Conman Who Sold the Eiffel Tower." *YouTube.* Video, 11:17. August 14.
    https://www.youtube.com/watch?v= YhYeSY6v8fl

15. FLETCHERWILSON. 2017. "My Advertising Is so Efficient It No Longer Works." *YouTube.* Video, 1:05:41. October 14.
    https://www.youtube.com/watch?v=ZtCG-Jo51d4

WEBSITES AND BLOGS

1. *San Today.gr*
   www.sansimera.gr

2. *Michael R. Virardi*
   www.michaelvirardi.com

3. DeMeré, Nichole Elizabeth, "The Power of Visual Storytelling: 15 Stunning Examples to Inspire You." *HubSpot* (blog), July 18, 2017.
   https://blog.hubspot.com/marketing/visual-storytelling-examples

4. Valuetainment. 2019. "15 Mistakes I Made as a CEO." *YouTube*. Video, 23:26. April 2.
   https://www.youtube.com/watch?v=UXJxr-vGo9o

5. "The couple buried in Delphi. Angelos Sikelianos and Eva Palmer, they loved each other and ancient Greece. They were bitter at the failure and separated, but were united by death." *mixanitouxronou*
   https://www.mixanitouxronou.gr/o-iperochos-erotas-tou-sikelianou-me-tin-eva-palmer-latrepsan-o-enas-ton-allon-ke-tin-archea-ellada-pikrathikan-apo-tin-apotichia-ke-chorisan-polla-chronia-meta-tafikan-mazi-stous-delfous/

6. "Mad Men". 2023. *Wikipedia: The Free Encyclopedia*. Last modified November 11.
   https://el.wikipedia.org/wiki/Mad_Men

7. TED. 2018. "How to build (and rebuild) trust | Frances Frei." *YouTube*. Video, 15:05. May 25.
   https://www.youtube.com/watch?v=pVeq-0dlqpk

8. *Wikipedia. The Free Encyclopedia.*
    https://el.wikipedia.org/
9. *Medium*
    https://medium.com/
10. *Alexa Blog* (blog)
    https://blog.alexa.com/10-buyer-persona-examples-help-create/
11. *BBC News*
    http://www.bbc.co.uk/
12. TEDx Talks. 2015. "The hidden truth about human connection | Dan Foxx | TEDxChelmsford." *YouTube*. Video, 18:29. August 20.
    https://www.youtube.com/watch?v=23vBLxJQk-Y
13. ThougtCatalyst. 2017. "The Secret Behind Coca-Cola Marketing Strategy." *YouTube*. Video, 8:15. October 5.
    https://www.youtube.com/watch?v=XhMVWzVXNNk
14. *mixanitouxronou*
    https: //www.mixanitouxronou.gr/
15. *Adweek*
    https://www.adweek.com/
16. *Fortune Greece*
    https://www.fortunegreece.com/photo-gallery/
17. *Newsbeast*
    https://www.newsbeast.gr/world/arthro/
18. *HistoryReport*
    http: //historyreport.gr/